The Behavior Problems Resource Kit

Forms and Procedures for Identification, Measurement, and Intervention

Michael J. Asher ○ Steven B. Gordon
Michael C. Selbst ○ Mark Cooperberg

Research Press ○ 2612 North Mattis Avenue ○ Champaign, Illinois 61822 ○ (800) 519-2707 ○ www.researchpress.com

Composition by Jeff Helgesen
Cover design by Linda Brown, Positive I.D. Graphic Design, Inc.
Printed by Malloy, Inc.

ISBN 13: 978-0-87822-633-7
Library of Congress Control Number 2009942806

CONTENTS

**Consequence Interventions: Controlling Positive and Negative
Reinforcement   158**

REPRODUCIBLE FORMS

Behavioral Interventions: Teaching Replacement Behaviors

Consequence Interventions: Controlling Positive and Negative Reinforcement

Appendix A

ACKNOWLEDGMENTS

We wish to acknowledge the countless number of parents, teachers, and children who have assisted us in the development of this book. The material here has gone through many revisions and has been field tested by many individuals. We are extremely grateful to those who have contributed. In many ways, the work here is best viewed as a work in progress. To all parents, teachers, and children—now and yet to come—we sincerely hope that these forms and interventions will lighten your load.

INTRODUCTION

Approximately one in four children and adolescents experience behavioral, developmental, emotional, or social and educational difficulties (Hibbs & Jenson, 2005). As clinical and school psychologists, our practice helps children and adolescents learn to overcome the problems they face in their lives. We concentrate on three important goals: accurately identifying problems, measuring severity, and implementing evidenced-based interventions. These critical steps improve the quality of life for children and adolescents and teach them the specific skills they need to overcome their difficulties.

As an extension of our clinical practice, we have developed behavior change projects that enlist mental health professionals, parents, and classroom teachers as partners. These projects are geared toward helping children reduce conflict, cope with problems, and reach their potential. Many of the forms, samples, and cases in this book are ones we use in our behavior change projects.

Our earlier books focused on children with attention deficit disorder: *Meeting the ADD Challenge: A Practical Guide for Teachers* (Gordon & Asher, 1994) and *The AD/HD Forms Book: Identification, Measurement, and Intervention* (Asher & Gordon, 1998). These books provided clinicians, parents, and teachers with tools to identify, measure, and intervene with the many challenges presented by children with AD/HD. Over the years, we applied the content of those books to help children with a range of disorders, which resulted in this text—a larger, more expansive toolbox of forms, questionnaires, sample completed forms, and interventions, for working with children with any diagnosis.

BEHAVIORAL AND COGNITIVE-BEHAVIORAL ORIENTATION

A significant body of evidence supports behavioral therapy and cognitive-behavioral therapy (CBT) as effective treatment modalities to address:

- internalizing disorders such as depression and anxiety (Bernstein, Bernat, Victor, & Layne, 2008; Hibbs & Jensen, 2004, TADS Team, 2007)

1

- externalizing disorders such as AD/HD, oppositional defiant disorder, and conduct disorder (Barkley, Edwards, Laneri, Fletcher, Metevia, 2001; Koegl, Farrington, Augimeri, & Day, 2008)

The resources in this book are grounded in this research attesting to the effectiveness of behavioral and cognitive-behavioral treatments.

ORGANIZATION OF THE TEXT

This book is divided into three main parts:

Part 1: Problem Identification

Part 2: Measurement and Functional Behavior Assessment

Part 3: Interventions

Each part begins with an overview of the purpose and use of the materials in that part. As the book proceeds, we provide an explanation of the purpose, content, and use of specific forms and procedures. In many cases, we include completed sample forms to assist you in using them.

Part 1: Problem Identification

Problem identification is always the first step in developing effective interventions. Therefore, Part 1 of the book is designed to facilitate gathering information to identify specific behaviors for change, assess their importance, and generate hypotheses regarding the function(s) of the problem behaviors.

Part 2: Measurement and Functional Behavioral Assessment

After a problem has been identified, measurement is the next task. A reliable baseline (i.e., preintervention) level is established to permit evaluation of the effectiveness of any interventions. The procedures and forms in Part 2 facilitate recording and organizing data regarding the problem behavior. These forms can be used before, during, and after an intervention to measure the extent and nature of changes. Problem behaviors can be measured by collecting data on frequency, duration, and intensity. Measurement contributes to an understanding of the settings, antecedent predictors, problem behaviors and maintaining consequences. Extensive data collection using an antecedent, behavior, and consequence (ABC) model permits the user to adapt interventions to personal, school, or organizational needs.

Part 3: Interventions

Interventions facilitate application of specific strategies to change behavior. This section begins by providing forms to document comprehensive behavior and social skills intervention plans. Following these forms, the material is grouped by antecedent, behavioral, and consequence interventions. It is essential to do as much as possible to reduce the need for socially maladaptive behaviors. *Antecedent interventions* allow those working with the child to make necessary changes prior to the occurrence of the challenging behavior. *Behavioral interventions* permit the replacement of the target or problem behavior. Included in this category are procedures and forms to teach skills to address social, emotional, developmental, functional, and educational issues and to promote coping strategies and positive change. *Consequence interventions* are designed to strengthen replacement behaviors and/or weaken inappropriate behaviors through the management of outcomes after the behaviors have taken place.

BEYOND THE CLINICAL ENVIRONMENT

Reaching beyond the clinical environment to involve parents and teachers is an important part of treatment. Training parents and teachers is highly useful in treating children and adolescents at home and in the classroom. School professionals such as counselors and school psychologists may use the cognitive strategies outlined in this book to assist students in making perceptual changes. Parents and teachers involved with children who are struggling with these disorders can benefit by using the forms in this book as their children engage in behavioral change.

The adults who live with and teach children with problems are often left with the task of taking a general concept (e.g., positive reinforcement, punishment, etc.) and figuring out how to apply it to their particular situation. This book provides the forms and information that facilitate the specific identification, measurement, and intervention of child/adolescent problems, for use in clinical settings, classrooms, and homes. Practitioners, teachers, and parents can use the well-established strategies and procedures presented in this book to begin taking action to improve the lives of children and adolescents who are struggling.

PART 1

PROBLEM IDENTIFICATION

The first step in developing an effective intervention program for a child or adolescent is identifying the problem. This involves gathering information about the child, describing problem behaviors, and understanding the situations when the problem behaviors occur. Identifying and describing the problem behaviors in detail provides critical information that brings to light the potential controlling variables.

CHILD HISTORY

To begin the process of problem identification, the parent or guardian completes the Child History Questionnaire (CHQ) to gather important information regarding the child's family demographics, developmental history, medical history, family history of psychological and behavioral problems, educational history, the history of the presenting problem, and intervention history.

IDENTIFY AND DESCRIBE BEHAVIORS AT HOME AND SCHOOL

The parent or guardian completes the Problem Behavior Questionnaire–Home (PBQ-H), and school personnel complete the Problem Behavior Questionnaire–School (PBQ-S). These forms precisely identify and describe the problem behaviors with which parents and school personnel are concerned. These forms require the problem behaviors to be operationally defined so that at least two independent observers can more reliably gather information regarding the occurrence or absence of the problem behavior. A sound operational definition for a problem behavior provides sufficient information for one to visualize the problem behavior, easily record the frequency of the behavior, determine when the behavior started and ended, and distinguish between the problem behavior and other behaviors the child displays.

IDENTIFY TASKS THAT CAUSE PROBLEMS

The Task Analysis Questionnaire: Home (TAQ-H) and Task Analysis Questionnaire–School (TAQ-S) assist the parent and school personnel in understanding situations in which the child is more or less likely to display compliance. The TAQ-H requires the parent or guardian to describe how the child responds to tasks at home. The form is divided into morning, after school, dinner, after dinner, and bedtime routines. The purpose is to gain a snapshot of a child's behavior and general level of functioning.

The TAQ-S assesses the student's problems in school by examining structured and unstructured classroom tasks and activities. Teachers and staff identify the specific profile of difficulties a child is experiencing and can address these challenging behaviors. Identified targeted areas can become the focus of the behavioral intervention planning. The TAQ-S covers the student's academic, behavioral, social, and functional abilities and provides an independent view of the student's behavior at school.

PINPOINT THE BEHAVIORS TO CHANGE

The final form in Part 1, the Pinpointing Form, identifies, or pinpoints, specific behaviors to be changed. These might be negative behaviors to decrease or positive behaviors to increase. This form identifies adaptive behaviors to direct attention toward positive interventions.

The questionnaires in Part 1 allow the clinician to gather information regarding the topography of the behavior, including the frequency, onset of the behavior, duration, severity, and location or setting. Additionally, circumstances contributing to the behavior may be considered through the respondents' careful consideration of various factors. These include antecedent conditions—situations and events that precede the problem behavior and may trigger the onset of the behavior and consequence conditions. Consequence conditions follow the problem behavior and may include responses displayed by the parent or guardian, school personnel, and other children, as well as natural and logical consequences the child experiences following the problem behavior. Consequence conditions may be viewed as positive, negative, or neutral. This depends on whether the consequence conditions increase or decrease the likelihood of the problem behavior's continuing or perhaps have no notable impact upon the problem behavior.

Child History Questionnaire

The Child History Questionnaire (CHQ) is a preintervention questionnaire that was developed to assess a child's history in a variety of areas. This questionnaire, completed by parents, is designed to examine the child's family demographics, developmental history, medical history, family history of psychological/behavioral problems, educational history, history of the presenting problem, and intervention history. By examining the child's history, the service provider can gain a fairly comprehensive understanding of the child in an efficient manner.

Mental health professionals and school personnel can use the CHQ as part of their initial assessment to provide important historical data that contribute to the provider's understanding, which in turn may influence interventions. This instrument should be used with students of all ages and can be filled out by adults who know the child well (e.g., parents, guardian, etc.) to gain a moving picture of history, rather than simply a "snapshot" of the child's current status. By completing the questionnaire, the parent or guardian is serving as the writer for the "movie" of the student's life history.

The Child History Questionnaire is divided into eight sections:

- family data
- presenting problem
- interventions
- developmental history
- child's medical history
- family psychological/medical history
- educational history
- additional information

Each completed section provides a view of the child's history leading up to the present. The CHQ is used as part of the preintervention assessment for each child prior to beginning treatment.

The greatest difficulty in completing this questionnaire is often a lack of information. Parents may have forgotten information about their child's developmental history, while other parents (such as adoptive parents) may be unaware of a child's family history. It is helpful to tell parents that this questionnaire is not a quiz to test them on how well they know their child; rather, it is a questionnaire that helps the clinician to gain a better understanding of the child's history, and that any provided information is helpful. In other cases, parents/guardians may feel uncomfortable sharing the family history of psychological difficulties. In such cases, the clinician should ask the parent or guardian to indicate which type of difficulties have been experienced by family members and whether the relative is a first degree relative (parent, sibling) or a second degree relative (grandparent, aunt, uncle, cousin), without identifying a specific individual. This helps some parents feel more comfortable with sharing important information in a child's history.

Child History Questionnaire

This background questionnaire will provide more than a snapshot of your child's current functioning. By completing this questionnaire, you are serving as a writer for the "movie" about your child's life history. Please complete the following to the best of your ability. Feel free to attach additional pages, if necessary, and add other information that you wish to share.

FAMILY DATA

Child's name _____ Date _____

Date of birth _____ Gender: ☐ female ☐ male

Age _____ Grade _____

Home address _____

_____

Form completed by (circle one):

mother   father   stepmother   stepfather   other (please explain) _____

Mother's name _____ Age _____ Highest level of education _____

Occupation _____

Telephone number: home _____work _____mobile _____

Father's name _____ Age _____ Highest level of education _____

Occupation _____

Telephone number: home _____work _____mobile _____

Stepparent's name _____ Age_____ Highest level of education _____

Occupation _____

Telephone number: home _____work _____mobile _____

Marital status of parents _____ Years married _____

From *The Behavior Problems Resource Kit,* © 2010 by Michael J. Asher, Steven B. Gordon, Michael C. Selbst, and Mark Cooperberg, Champaign, IL: Research Press (800-519-2707, www.researchpress.com)

List all people living in household.

Name	Relationship to child	Age
_____	_____	_____
_____	_____	_____
_____	_____	_____
_____	_____	_____
_____	_____	_____

List the names and ages of any brothers or sisters living outside the home. _____

_____

What is the primary language spoken in the home? _____

What other languages are spoken in the home? _____

PRESENTING PROBLEM

Briefly describe your child's most significant current difficulties.

_____

_____

_____

_____

How long has this problem(s) been of concern to you? _____

When was the problem(s) first noticed? _____ By whom? _____

What factors do you believe may have contributed to the problem(s)? _____

_____

_____

What seems to make the problem(s) worse? _____

_____

What seems to reduce the problem(s)? _____

_____

Who referred you here? What is his/her relationship to your child and/or position (pediatrician, teacher, tutor, uncle, etc.)?

_____

INTERVENTIONS

Has the child received any prior evaluations or consultations for this problem or any other issues?   ☐ Yes ☐ No

If yes, when and with whom? _____ (Please provide a copy of any reports.)

Has the child ever been hospitalized for psychiatric/psychological problems?   ☐ Yes   ☐ No

If yes, when, where, for how long, and for what reasons? _____

Is the child on any medication at this time?   ☐ Yes   ☐ No

If yes, what kind of medication, dosage, who prescribed it, and when? _____

_____

Has the child been on any other medications in the past?   ☐ Yes   ☐ No

Explain _____

_____

Who is prescribing the medication? _____

What is the prescriber's specialization (pediatrician, psychiatrist, etc.)? _____

Is your child currently involved in therapy/counseling?   ☐ Yes   ☐ No

If yes, where, with whom, for how long? _____

What is the primary problem to be addressed by therapy/counseling?_____

Has your child had any prior therapy/counseling?   ☐ Yes   ☐ No

Please list any diagnoses provided. _____

By whom? _____ Date _____

DEVELOPMENTAL HISTORY

During pregnancy

Were there any complications?   ☐ Yes   ☐ No   If yes, describe. _____

_____

Was the mother on medication?　☐ Yes　☐ No

If yes, what kind? _____

Did the mother smoke?　☐ Yes　☐ No

If yes, how many cigarettes each day? _____

Did the mother drink alcoholic beverages?　☐ Yes　☐ No

If yes, what did she drink and how much per day? _____

Did the mother use drugs?　☐ Yes　☐ No

If yes, what kind and how frequently? _____

Birth

Was the child born full-term?　☐ Yes　☐ No (premature) _____

If no, how many weeks premature? _____

Was a Caesarian-section performed?　☐ Yes　☐ No　If yes, why? _____

Were forceps used during delivery?　☐ Yes　☐ No

What was the child's birth weight? _____

Were there any birth defects or complications?　☐ Yes　☐ No

If yes, please describe. _____

Early Development

Were there any feeding problems?　☐ Yes　☐ No

If yes, please describe. _____

Were there any sleeping problems?　☐ Yes　☐ No

If yes, please describe. _____

As an infant, was the child quiet?　☐ Yes　☐ No

Were you told the child had colic?　☐ Yes　☐ No

As an infant, did the child like to be held? ☐ Yes ☐ No

As an infant, was the child alert? ☐ Yes ☐ No

Were there any problems in the growth and development of the child during the first few years? ☐ Yes ☐ No

If yes, please describe. _____

Following is a list of infant and preschool behaviors. Please indicate the age at which your child first demonstrated each behavior. If you are not certain of the age but have some idea, write the age followed by a question mark. If you have no idea the age at which the behavior occurred, please write a question mark.

Behavior	Age (months)	Behavior	Age (months)
Showed response to parent	_____	Put several words together	_____
Rolled over	_____	Dressed self	_____
Babbled	_____	Spoke first word	_____
Became toilet trained	_____	Stayed dry at night	_____
Crawled	_____	Walked alone	_____
Fed self	_____	Rode a bike without training wheels	_____

CHILD'S MEDICAL HISTORY

Place a checkmark next to any illness or condition that your child has had. When you check an item, also note the approximate date (or age) of the illness or condition. Please do not spend too much time searching for the dates/ages if you are unsure.

Illness/Condition	Date(s)/ age(s)	Illness/condition	Date(s)/ age(s)
☐ Dizziness/fainting spells	_____	☐ Extreme tiredness	_____
☐ Convulsions/seizures/epilepsy	_____	☐ High fever	_____
☐ Frequent/severe headaches	_____	☐ Allergy	_____
☐ Injuries to head	_____	☐ Asthma	_____
☐ Broken bones	_____	☐ Vision problems	_____
☐ Hospitalizations	_____	☐ Suicide attempt	_____
☐ High blood pressure	_____	☐ Operations	_____

☐ Ear infections   _____   ☐ Hearing problems   _____

☐ Loss of consciousness   _____   ☐ Other   _____

Does your child wear glasses, contact lenses, or a hearing aid?   ☐ Yes   ☐ No

If yes, please specify. _____

Does your child take any medications to address a medical condition?   ☐ Yes   ☐ No

If yes, please specify. _____

FAMILY PSYCHOLOGICAL/MEDICAL HISTORY

Place a checkmark next to any illness or condition that any member of the family has had (parents, siblings, grandparents, aunts/uncles). When you check an item, please note the member's relationship to the child.

Condition

Relationship to child
(please specify maternal/paternal)

☐ Language/learning problems   _____

☐ Behavior problems (in school, with law)   _____

☐ Attention-deficit/hyperactivity disorder   _____

☐ Depression   _____

☐ Bipolar disorder   _____

☐ Anxiety disorder(s)   _____

☐ Eating disorder   _____

☐ Pervasive developmental disorder (autism, Asperger's disorder, PDD-NOS)   _____

☐ Psychosis   _____

☐ Sleep disorder   _____

☐ Alcoholism   _____

☐ Drug abuse   _____

☐ Suicide or suicide attempt   _____

☐ Other psychological problem(s)   _____

   (Please explain.) _____

☐ Medical problems (e.g., high blood pressure,   _____
   diabetes, cancer, heart trouble)

Please list any psychological or medical treatments that relatives have received, and the effectiveness of the treatment, if known.

_____

_____

EDUCATIONAL HISTORY

Please provide any prior reports, IEPs, evaluations, report cards, school achievement test results, examples of academic work, physician telephone numbers, etc.

Child's current school _____ Grade _____ District _____

Please list additional schools, day care, preschool, etc. that your child has attended.

Dates (from/to)	School grade (if applicable)	School district
_____	_____	_____
_____	_____	_____
_____	_____	_____

Place a checkmark next to any educational problems that your child currently exhibits.

☐ difficulty with reading   ☐ difficulty with other subjects (please list)

☐ difficulty with arithmetic   _____

☐ difficulty with writing   ☐ difficulty with spelling

☐ does not like school   ☐ refuses to attend school

☐ difficulty on tests   ☐ difficulty completing daily homework

☐ difficulty with classroom behaviors   ☐ difficulty completing larger projects

☐ inconsistent grades   ☐ a recent drop in grades/performance

☐ difficulty with teachers, school staff   ☐ difficulties with other students

Please provide additional information or comments with respect to the items you checked.

_____

_____

Is your child in a special education class?   ☐ Yes   ☐ No

If yes, what type of class? _____

Has your child ever been held back (repeated a grade)?   ☐ Yes   ☐ No

If yes, what grade and why? _____

Has your child ever received special tutoring or therapy/counseling in school?   ☐ Yes   ☐ No

Has your child ever received special tutoring or therapy/counseling outside of school?
☐ Yes   ☐ No

If yes to either, please describe (with whom, how often, subjects, duration of work).

_____

ADDITIONAL INFORMATION

What disciplinary techniques do you use when your child behaves inappropriately? Place a checkmark next to each technique that you usually use.

☐ ignore problem behavior   ☐ time out/send child to his/her room

☐ scold child   ☐ spank child

☐ attempt to reason with child   ☐ take away desirable activity or object

☐ threaten child   (specify) _____

☐ redirect child's interest   ☐ other technique (describe) _____

                                                          _____

Which disciplinary techniques are usually effective? _____

With which type of problem(s) are they effective? _____

Which disciplinary techniques are usually ineffective? _____

With which type of problem(s) are they ineffective? _____

What are your child's favorite activities? _____

_____

What activities would you like your child to engage in more often at this time? _____

_____

What activities does your child like least? _____

Has your child ever been in trouble with the law? ☐ Yes ☐ No

If yes, please explain. _____

Has your child witnessed or been involved in any traumatic events (death, near-death, abuse)?
☐ Yes ☐ No

If yes, please explain._____

_____

What have you found to be most the most satisfactory ways of helping your child? _____

_____

What are your child's assets or strengths? _____

_____

Please list any other information that you think may help us in working with your child.

_____

_____

_____

Thank you very much for your time and for your cooperation.

Problem Behavior Questionnaire–Home

The Problem Behavior Questionnaire–Home (PBQ–H), completed by parents or guardians, is a preintervention questionnaire developed to assess a child's problem behavior. This instrument should be used with children of all ages and can be filled out by one or more parents to gain a detailed understanding of a child's problem behavior, including antecedent and consequential conditions and the effect of previous interventions. If the clinician prefers, guardians or other adults who have a solid understanding of the child may also complete the PBQ–H.

Mental health professionals and school personnel can use this instrument as part of their initial assessment of the identified child. This questionnaire may provide important behavioral data that shape the provider's view of the child's behavior, which in turn helps to shape the resulting interventions.

The PBQ–H is divided into several sections:

- the child's strengths
- presenting problem
- interventions that have been tried
- information related to reinforcers and replacement behaviors

The greatest difficulty in completing this questionnaire is often a lack of available information. Parents may be unaware of antecedent conditions or the consequences that follow the behavior. Furthermore, they may have difficulty coming to a clear conclusion about previous interventions. The clinician should ask the respondent to fill in as much information as they can, but acknowledge that they may not be able to provide an answer to every question. It is also helpful to tell parents that this questionnaire is not a test on how well they know their child; rather, it is a questionnaire that helps the clinician to gain a better understanding of the child's behavior, and that any information they can provide is helpful.

Your completion of this questionnaire will provide valuable information regarding your child's presenting behavior, including circumstances contributing to the target behavior(s), replacement behaviors to consider, and additional relevant information.

Child's name _____ Date _____

Date of birth _____ Gender: ☐ female ☐ male

Age _____ Grade _____

Form completed by _____

Relationship to child _____

CHILD'S STRENGTHS

Briefly describe the child's strengths.

_____

_____

_____

_____

PRESENTING PROBLEM

1. Briefly describe problem behaviors that need to be changed. Please be very specific—for example, instead of "anger," write "hits his sister."

_____

_____

_____

_____

2. How long has the problem been a concern? _____

When was the problem first noticed? _____

By whom? _____

3. Please place a checkmark next to all factors that may contribute to the problem behavior. For any factor you have checked, please circle all specific items that may be relevant.

☐ academic (spelling, reading, writing, math, auditory processing, memory, organization, planning skills)

☐ physiological or medical (e.g., sleep, medication, hunger/thirst, vision, hearing, health, limitations)

☐ mental health (e.g., emotional problems, AD/HD, depression, anxiety, adjustment problems)

☐ possible substance use (please specify _____)

☐ family issues (e.g., divorce/separation, mental health, medical)

☐ classroom environment (lighting, seating arrangement, noise level, proximity to other children, clothing sensitivity)

☐ other (please explain _____)

4. What is the estimated frequency of the target behavior? (e.g., five times a day, three times a week)

_____

5. What is the duration of the target behavior (i.e., for how long does it typically occur)?

_____

6. Antecedents

a. What circumstances, situations, or events may trigger the problem behavior(s)?

_____

_____

_____

b. What circumstances rarely set the occasion for the problem behavior to occur?

_____

_____

_____

7. Consequences

a. What do you do when your child displays the problem behavior?

_____

_____

b. What do other children do when your child displays the problem behavior?

_____

_____

8. Impact of problem behavior

a. What impact does the problem behavior have on the child's education?

_____

_____

b. What impact does the problem behavior have on the child's relationship with adults?

_____

_____

c. What impact does the problem behavior have on the child's relationship with peers?

_____

_____

INTERVENTIONS THAT HAVE BEEN TRIED

1. What specifically has been done when the child displays the problem behavior?

☐ ignore problem behavior ☐ attempt to reason with child

☐ verbally reprimand ☐ redirect child's interest

☐ remove privileges ☐ reinforce appropriate behavior

☐ time out ☐ detention

☐ suspension ☐ parent contact (e.g., letter, telephone call, conference)

☐ other (describe) _____

2. Describe the effectiveness of any interventions.

_____

_____

3. Have there been prior evaluations/consultations? ☐ Yes ☐ No

If yes, explain. _____

4. Is the child prescribed any medication? ☐ Yes ☐ No

If yes, explain. _____

5. Is the child currently or has the child previously been involved in therapy or counseling?
   ☐ Yes   ☐ No

   If yes, explain. _____

6. Is the child receiving special education services?   ☐ Yes   ☐ No

   If yes, explain. _____

7. Is the child receiving a 504 Accommodation Plan?   ☐ Yes   ☐ No

   If yes, explain. _____

8. Has the child ever been retained or repeated a grade?   ☐ Yes   ☐ No

   If yes, explain. _____

OTHER INFORMATION

1. What activities does the child enjoy or prefer (e.g., sports, computers, reading, television)?

   _____

   _____

2. What other activities or rewards might the child enjoy (e.g., music, certain foods, stickers, certificates, recognition)?

   _____

   _____

3. How does the child feel about his/her behavior?

   _____

   _____

4. Are there any additional concerns or other relevant information regarding your child?

   _____

   _____

REPLACEMENT BEHAVIORS

Describe the behaviors or skills that need to be developed or strengthened (e.g., controlling anger, expressing feelings more appropriately, asking for help, problem solving).

_____

_____

_____

Problem Behavior Questionnaire–School

The Problem Behavior Questionnaire (PBQ–S) is a preintervention questionnaire that provides critical information about the student's problem behavior in school. This questionnaire is designed to examine:

- an operational definition of the problem target behavior
- the topography of the behavior (i.e., frequency, duration, severity)
- circumstances contributing to the target behavior(s)
- replacement behaviors to consider
- additional relevant information

This questionnaire is completed prior to the initial consult by teachers or other school personnel, including paraprofessionals, case managers, special education directors, school-based therapists or counselors, related service providers (i.e., speech language pathologists, occupational therapists, physical therapists), and administrators. Examining the child's behavior gives the service provider a comprehensive understanding of the student's problem behavior, strengths, and responses to previous interventions prior to the initial consult.

In addition, this questionnaire may be used by child study teams, psychologists, and clinicians as part of their initial assessment of the identified child. This behavioral data shape the clinician's understanding of the student's behavior and allows for decisions about appropriate interventions.

This instrument can be used with students of all ages to gain a detailed understanding of the problem behavior, including antecedent and consequential conditions and the effect of previous interventions. The form needs to be completed only once (i.e., during the assessment stage of the intervention process).

The PBQ–S is divided into the following sections:

- demographic information
- performance with school work, homework, and participation in school
- strengths
- presenting problem
- interventions that have been tried
- information related to reinforcers and replacement behaviors
- a checklist for accommodations and modifications

The greatest difficulty in completing this questionnaire is often a lack of information. Teachers may be unaware of the topography of the behavior at school for several reasons. There may be a lack of data collection, trouble attending sufficiently to one student within a classroom, or difficulty conceptualizing the behavior beyond simply observing the target behavior. The respondent (the student's teacher or parent, for example) may not have considered the antecedent conditions or the consequences that follow the behavior. Therefore, teachers may have difficulty arriving at a clear conclusion about previous interventions.

The clinician should ask the respondent to fill in as much information as they can, but acknowledge that they may not be able to provide an answer to every question. If a teacher is completing the questionnaire, the clinician might tell the teacher that this is not a test on how well they know their student or the student's behavior. Rather, this is a questionnaire that helps the clinician to obtain a better understanding of the student's behavior, and that any information they can provide is helpful.

In some cases, teachers may feel uncomfortable sharing their previous interventions since they may be acknowledging ineffective strategies or those that they feel were unethical (e.g., excessive use of time-out procedures, yelling at student). In such cases, the clinician can ask the teacher to indicate what the perceived effectiveness of such interventions were, and the clinician can provide an empathic response ("Teaching is very challenging and can be very frustrating"). At the same time, the clinician can provide psychoeducation: "I can understand how challenging the student's behavior may be for you. It sounds like ultimately you did not find those strategies to be effective, despite some improvement in the short term. We will work together to understand this student's behavior and to develop a more comprehensive plan."

Please complete this form for the student named below. Your input is extremely valuable as part of this assessment. This will assist us in understanding the student's strengths and needs, and in providing appropriate recommendations to improve the student's educational performance. When describing a problem behavior, please be as specific as possible by giving a clear operational definition.

Student's name _____ Date _____

Date of birth _____ Gender: ☐ female   ☐ male

Age _____ Grade _____

Teacher's name _____

Type of teacher

☐ Regular education teacher   ☐ Special education teacher   ☐ Paraprofessional

☐ Other _____

Subject taught _____

Type of classroom

☐ Regular education classroom   ☐ Resource center   ☐ Self-contained classroom

☐ Other _____

Name of school _____

STUDENT'S ACADEMIC PERFORMANCE

Current grade _____ Quiz grades _____

Test grades _____ Other _____

Tests and quizzes

Are tests and quizzes generally completed within the allowed time?

☐ Yes ☐ No Comments _____

Homework

Does the student complete homework on a regular basis?

☐ Yes ☐ No Comments _____

Are assignments handed in on time?

☐ Yes ☐ No Comments _____

What is the general quality of the assignments?

☐ Below average ☐ Average ☐ Above average

Class participation

Is the student prepared for class with appropriate materials?

☐ Yes ☐ No Comments _____

Does the student typically participate in class?

☐ Yes ☐ No Comments _____

Does the student seek help when needed?

☐ Yes ☐ No Comments _____

During small group assignments, is the student actively engaged?

☐ Yes ☐ No Comments _____

During small group assignments, does the student display appropriate social interactions?

☐ Yes ☐ No Comments _____

STUDENT'S STRENGTHS

Briefly describe the student's strengths.

_____

_____

_____

_____

PRESENTING PROBLEM

1. Briefly describe the behaviors that need to be changed. Please be very specific—for example, instead of "anger," write "hits classmate."

   _____

   _____

   _____

   _____

2. How long has the problem been a concern? _____

   When was the problem first noticed? _____

   By whom? _____

3. Please place a checkmark next to all factors that may contribute to the problem behavior. For any factor you check, please circle all specific items that may be relevant.

   ☐ academic (spelling, reading, writing, mathematics, auditory processing, memory, organization, planning skills)

   ☐ physiological or medical (e.g., sleep, medication, hunger/thirst, vision, hearing, health, limitations)

   ☐ mental health (e.g., emotional problems, AD/HD, depression, anxiety, adjustment problems)

   ☐ possible substance use (please specify) _____

   ☐ family issues (e.g., divorce/separation, mental health, medical)

   ☐ classroom environment (lighting, seating arrangement, noise level, proximity to other children, clothing sensitivity)

   ☐ other (please explain) _____

4. What is the estimated frequency of the target behavior? (e.g., five times a day, three times a week)

   _____

5. What is the duration of the target behavior? (i.e., for how long does it typically occur?)

_____

6. Antecedents

   a. What circumstances, situations, or events may trigger the problem behavior(s)?

_____

_____

_____

   b. What circumstances *rarely* set the occasion for the problem behavior to occur?

_____

_____

_____

7. Consequences

   a. What do you do when the student displays the problem behavior?

_____

_____

_____

   b. What do other students do when the student displays the problem behavior?

_____

_____

_____

8. Impact of problem behavior

   a. What impact does the problem behavior have on the student's education?

_____

_____

_____

   b. What impact does the problem behavior have on the student's relationship with adults?

_____

_____

_____

c. What impact does the problem behavior have on the student's relationship with peers?

_____

_____

_____

INTERVENTIONS TRIED

1. What specifically has been done when the student displays the problem behavior?

☐ ignore problem behavior   ☐ attempt to reason with student

☐ verbal reprimand   ☐ redirect student's interest

☐ remove privileges   ☐ reinforce appropriate behavior

☐ time out   ☐ detention

☐ suspension   ☐ parent contact (e.g., letter, telephone call, conference)

☐ other (describe) _____

2. Describe the effectiveness of any interventions. _____

_____

3. Have there been prior evaluations/consultations?   ☐ Yes   ☐ No

If yes, then explain. _____

4. Is the student prescribed any medication?   ☐ Yes   ☐ No

If yes, explain. _____

5. Is the student currently or has the student previously been involved in therapy or counseling?
☐ Yes   ☐ No

If yes, explain. _____

6. Is the student receiving special education services?   ☐ Yes   ☐ No

If yes, explain. _____

7. Is the student receiving a 504 Accommodation Plan?   ☐ Yes   ☐ No

If yes, explain. _____

8. Has the student ever been retained or repeated a grade?   ☐ Yes   ☐ No

If yes, explain. _____

OTHER INFORMATION

1. What activities does the student enjoy or prefer (e.g., sports, computers, reading, television)?

_____

_____

2. What other activities or rewards might the student enjoy (e.g., music, certain foods, stickers, certificates, recognition)?

_____

_____

3. How does the student feel about his/her behavior?

_____

_____

4. Are there any additional concerns or other relevant information regarding this student?

_____

_____

REPLACEMENT BEHAVIORS

Describe the behaviors or skills that need to be developed or strengthened (e.g., controlling anger, expressing feelings more appropriately, asking for help, problem solving).

_____

_____

_____

ACCOMODATIONS AND MODIFICATIONS

What accommodations, modifications, or instructional supports, if any, do you feel are appropriate for this student? Please check all that apply and feel free to write in additional supports.

Currently receiving	Not receiving but could be helpful	
☐	☐	extended time for tests and/or quizzes
☐	☐	extended time for homework assignments
☐	☐	extended time for long-term assignments
☐	☐	breaking long-term assignments into smaller parts

Currently receiving	Not receiving but could be helpful	
☐	☐	preferential seating
☐	☐	study guide
☐	☐	peer buddy to check in with
☐	☐	outline of lecture during class
☐	☐	graphic organizer for writing assignments
☐	☐	homework planner to be reviewed by staff and parent and signed
☐	☐	morning and/or afternoon check-in for organization of desk and book bag
☐	☐	morning and/or afternoon check-in regarding student's mood and/or behavior
☐	☐	repeating and rephrasing questions
☐	☐	amplification system to increase volume of staff's voice
☐	☐	assistive technology for class assignments (e.g., keyboard, audiotape)
☐	☐	planned movement breaks
☐	☐	more frequent behavior-specific praise compared to typical student
☐	☐	more individualized instruction or assistance compared to typical student
☐	☐	visual prompts to help student write neatly (e.g., spacing, staying on lines)
☐	☐	use of hands-on materials (manipulatives)
☐	☐	reading or talking aloud to improve comprehension
☐	☐	extra set of books at home
☐	☐	color-coded folders
☐	☐	checklists for completion of assignments (e.g., topic sentence, spelling/punctuation)
☐	☐	extended time for homework assignments
☐	☐	other _____
☐	☐	other _____

Task Analysis Questionnaire–Home

The Task Analysis Questionnaire–Home (TAQ–H) is a 32-item preintervention questionnaire to assess the problems in the home. This questionnaire is filled out by the child's parents/guardians/caretakers to provide the best picture of home behaviors. The TAQ–H examines structured home tasks and activities as well as events in unstructured settings. Examining these activities and settings identifies the specific profile of difficulties a child is experiencing so that these challenging behaviors can be addressed.

Clinicians can use this instrument as a baseline assessment of the problems that the child may be experiencing. Consequently, the identified targeted areas can become the focus of behavioral intervention planning.

This instrument should be used with children who are school-age (pre-K through grade 12). One or more adults can complete this questionnaire to gain a picture of how a child functions and behaves during a typical day or with specific adults.

The TAQ–H is divided into five domains:

- morning routine
- after-school routine
- dinner time
- after dinner time
- bedtime routine

The adult completing the form is asked to indicate the degree to which the child complies with the task on a three-point scale (i.e., never, sometimes, very often) and then indicate the importance of the task (i.e., not important, important, critical).

The purpose of this instrument is to gain a snapshot of a child's behavior and general level of functioning. Therefore, this questionnaire can be used many times during the course of treatment to establish a baseline (i.e., preintervention level) and then to evaluate the effectiveness of the behavioral intervention planning that may emerge. Also, this questionnaire can be used each year by a clinician to continuously assess the child's overall development.

The greatest difficulty facing the clinician is often deciding where to begin intervention. The TAQ–H provides an assessment of severity and importance that facilitates the clinician's decision-making process.

Task Analysis Questionnaire–Home

The purpose of this questionnaire is to provide critical information regarding your child's compliance with various tasks throughout the day. This is important to better understand parent-child interactions, circumstances in which there is more/less compliance, and the degree of importance you place upon each task.

Child's name _____ Date _____

Date of birth _____ Gender: ☐ female ☐ male

Age _____ Grade _____

Form completed by _____

Relationship to child _____

Directions

1. Please consider your child's behavior over the past 30 days while reading each item.

   • If the item is *not applicable,* circle N/A.

   • If your child *never* displays the skill, circle 0.

   • If your child *sometimes* displays the skill, circle 1.

   • If your child *very often* displays this skill, circle 2.

2. Please also rate how important you believe the skill is as part of your child's overall development.

   • If the item is *not applicable*, circle N/A.

   • If the skill is *not important,* circle 0.

   • If the skill is *important*, circle 1.

   • If the skill is *critical*, circle 2.

	How often is the task displayed with compliance (i.e., child completes task without conflict and within parent/guardian's expected time frame)?				How important is the task to you?			
		Never	Sometimes	Very Often		Not important	Important	Critical
	N/A	0	1	2	N/A	0	1	2

Morning Routine

1. Gets out of bed	N/A	0	1	2	N/A	0	1	2
2. Uses bathroom for brushing teeth, washing, and toileting	N/A	0	1	2	N/A	0	1	2
3 Gets dressed	N/A	0	1	2	N/A	0	1	2
4. Eats breakfast	N/A	0	1	2	N/A	0	1	2
5. Takes medication and/or vitamins	N/A	0	1	2	N/A	0	1	2
6. Is prepared with all materials for school	N/A	0	1	2	N/A	0	1	2
7. Leaves the house on time	N/A	0	1	2	N/A	0	1	2
8. Other (Please write in.)	N/A	0	1	2	N/A	0	1	2

_____

_____

Total Score

Number of items _____

Total score _____

Number of items _____

Total score _____

After-School Routine

1. Arrives home in timely manner after school	N/A	0	1	2	N/A	0	1	2
2. Brings home all necessary materials from school	N/A	0	1	2	N/A	0	1	2
3. Begins homework assignments in a timely manner	N/A	0	1	2	N/A	0	1	2
4. Remains on task while working	N/A	0	1	2	N/A	0	1	2
5. Completes homework assignments in a timely manner	N/A	0	1	2	N/A	0	1	2

	How often is the task displayed with compliance?				How important is the task to you?			
		Never	Sometimes	Very Often		Not important	Important	Critical
	N/A	0	1	2	N/A	0	1	2
6. Puts away materials after completing assignments	N/A	0	1	2	N/A	0	1	2
7. Respects others in the house who are working	N/A	0	1	2	N/A	0	1	2
8. Writes assigments in agenda	N/A	0	1	2	N/A	0	1	2
9. Other (Please write in.)	N/A	0	1	2	N/A	0	1	2

_____

_____

Total Score　　　　Number of items _____　　　Number of items _____

　　　　　　　　　　　Total score _____　　　　Total score _____

Dinner Time

	How often				How important			
1. Sits down at dinner table in a timely manner	N/A	0	1	2	N/A	0	1	2
2. Displays appropriate table manners throughout the meal	N/A	0	1	2	N/A	0	1	2
3. Remains seated throughout the meal	N/A	0	1	2	N/A	0	1	2
4. Engages in reciprocal conversation with family members	N/A	0	1	2	N/A	0	1	2
5. Respects others throughout the meal	N/A	0	1	2	N/A	0	1	2
6. Eats an adequate amount of food	N/A	0	1	2	N/A	0	1	2
7. Helps clean up after meal	N/A	0	1	2	N/A	0	1	2
8. Other (Please write in.)	N/A	0	1	2	N/A	0	1	2

_____

_____

Total Score　　　　Number of items _____　　　Number of items _____

　　　　　　　　　　　Total score _____　　　　Total score _____

	How often is the task displayed with compliance?				How important is the task to you?			
	Never	Sometimes	Very Often		Not important	Important	Critical	
	N/A	0	1	2	N/A	0	1	2

After Dinner Time

1. Engages in appropriate leisure-time activity	N/A	0	1	2	N/A	0	1	2
2. Respects others in the house and neighborhood	N/A	0	1	2	N/A	0	1	2
3. Ends leisure-time activity within timely manner	N/A	0	1	2	N/A	0	1	2
4. Other (Please write in.)	N/A	0	1	2	N/A	0	1	2

_____

_____

Total Score

Number of items _____

Total score _____

Number of items _____

Total score _____

Bedtime Routine

1. Brushes teeth within timely manner	N/A	0	1	2	N/A	0	1	2
2. Uses toilet within timely manner	N/A	0	1	2	N/A	0	1	2
3. Bathes or showers within timely manner	N/A	0	1	2	N/A	0	1	2
4. Gest dressed in pajamas or nightgown in timely manner	N/A	0	1	2	N/A	0	1	2
5. Gest in bed within timely manner	N/A	0	1	2	N/A	0	1	2
6. Respects others in the house	N/A	0	1	2	N/A	0	1	2
7. Turns out lights within a timely manner	N/A	0	1	2	N/A	0	1	2
8. Other (Please write in.)	N/A	0	1	2	N/A	0	1	2

_____

_____

Total Score

Number of items _____

Total score _____

Number of items _____

Total score _____

SCORING

	How often is the task displayed with compliance?		How important is the task to you?	
	Number of items	**Total score**	**Number of items**	**Total score**
Morning routine	————	————	————	————
After-school routine	————	————	————	————
Dinner time	————	————	————	————
After dinner time	————	————	————	————
Bedtime routine	————	————	————	————
Total scores	**Number of items**	**Total score**	**Number of items**	**Total score**
	————	————	————	————

Task Analysis Questionnaire–School

The Task Analysis Questionnaire—School (TAQ–S) is a preintervention questionnaire developed to assess the student's problems in school. Classroom teachers and school staff complete this questionnaire to gain the best picture of a student's school behaviors. The TAQ–S examines structured classroom tasks and activities as well as unstructured setting events that students are expected to participate in. By examining these activities and settings, teachers and staff can identify the specific profile of difficulties a child is experiencing and can address these challenging behaviors.

Child study teams, psychologists, and clinicians working with schools and students can use this instrument as part of their baseline assessment of the problems that the student may be experiencing. Consequently, identified targeted areas can become the focus of the behavioral intervention planning.

This instrument should be used with students who are school-age (pre-K through grade 12). One or more school personnel may complete the form to gain a picture of how a student functions and behaves across a typical school day or with specific teachers and subjects.

The TAQ–S is divided into two parts: structured and unstructured tasks, and settings. There are 15 questions that examine how the student has adapted to classroom expectations. They examine the student's academic, behavioral, social and functional abilities and allow the respondent to provide an independent view of the student's behavior at school. There are also 10 questions that examine how the student behaves with less supervision and the problems that may arise outside of the teacher's supervision.

The purpose of this instrument is to gain a snapshot of a student's behavior and general level of functioning. Therefore, the TAQ–S can be used many times during the course of treatment, first for baseline problem areas and then to evaluate the effectiveness of the behavioral intervention planning. This form can be used each year to continuously assess any changes in the student's ability to adapt to school demands.

The purpose of this questionnaire is to provide critical information regarding compliance with various tasks that you may expect from the student throughout the day. This information is important to better understand teacher-student interactions, circumstances in which there is more/less compliance, and the degree of importance you place upon each task.

Child's name _____ Date _____

Date of birth _____ Gender: ☐ female ☐ male

Age _____ Grade _____

Form completed by _____

Relationship to child _____

Directions

1. Please consider the student's behavior over the past 30 days while reading each item.

   - If the item is *not applicable*, circle N/A.
   - If the student *never* displays the skill, circle 0.
   - If the student *sometimes* displays the skill, circle 1.
   - If the student *very often* displays this skill, circle 2.

2. Please rate how important you believe the skill is as part of the student's overall development.

   - If the item is *not applicable,* circle N/A.
   - If the skill is *not important,* then circle 0.
   - If the skill is *important,* circle 1.
   - If the skill is *critical,* circle 2.

	How often is the task displayed with compliance (i.e., child completes task without conflict and within parent/guardian's expected time frame)?				How important is the task to you?			
		Never	Sometimes	Very Often		Not important	Important	Critical
	N/A	0	1	2	N/A	0	1	2

Structured Activities

1. Arrives at school	N/A	0	1	2	N/A	0	1	2
2. Follows morning routine	N/A	0	1	2	N/A	0	1	2
3. Completes morning routine	N/A	0	1	2	N/A	0	1	2
4. Manages and organizes needed materials	N/A	0	1	2	N/A	0	1	2
5. Initiates deskwork with class	N/A	0	1	2	N/A	0	1	2
6. Participates in cooperative work groups	N/A	0	1	2	N/A	0	1	2
7. Behaves appropriately during free time in the classroom	N/A	0	1	2	N/A	0	1	2
8. Behaves appropriately during classroom instruction	N/A	0	1	2	N/A	0	1	2
9. Participates in school special events	N/A	0	1	2	N/A	0	1	2
10. Participates in resource or basic skills classes	N/A	0	1	2	N/A	0	1	2
11. Transitions appropriately between classes or activities	N/A	0	1	2	N/A	0	1	2
12. Maintains desk or school locker	N/A	0	1	2	N/A	0	1	2
13. Packs up needed materials at the end of the day	N/A	0	1	2	N/A	0	1	2
14. Completes homework assignments	N/A	0	1	2	N/A	0	1	2
15. Uses school agenda or assignment book	N/A	0	1	2	N/A	0	1	2

Task Analysis Questionnaire–School (page 2 of 4)

	How often is the task displayed with compliance?				How important is the task to you?			
		Never	Sometimes	Very Often		Not important	Important	Critical
	N/A	0	1	2	N/A	0	1	2
16. Other (Please write in.)	N/A	0	1	2	N/A	0	1	2

_____

_____

Total Score   Number of items _____   Number of items _____

                 Total score _____   Total score _____

Unstructured Activities

1. Participates appropriately at lunch	N/A	0	1	2	N/A	0	1	2
2. Participates appropriately at recess	N/A	0	1	2	N/A	0	1	2
3. Moves through hallways without disturbing others	N/A	0	1	2	N/A	0	1	2
4. Uses the bathroom appropriately	N/A	0	1	2	N/A	0	1	2
5. Respect others (e.g., school assistants)	N/A	0	1	2	N/A	0	1	2
6. Eats an adequate amount of food	N/A	0	1	2	N/A	0	1	2
7. Behaves appropriately at school assemblies	N/A	0	1	2	N/A	0	1	2
8. Resects others during activities	N/A	0	1	2	N/A	0	1	2
9. Waits quietly before school	N/A	0	1	2	N/A	0	1	2
10. On the school bus to and from school	N/A	0	1	2	N/A	0	1	2
11. Other (Please write in.)	N/A	0	1	2	N/A	0	1	2

_____

_____

Total Score   Number of items _____   Number of items _____

                 Total score _____   Total score _____

SCORING

	How often is the task displayed with compliance?		How important is the task to you?	
	Number of items	Total score	Number of items	Total score
Structured activities	_____	_____	_____	_____
Unstructured activities	_____	_____	_____	_____
Total scores	Number of items	Total score	Number of items	Total score
	_____	_____	_____	_____

Pinpointing

Pinpointing means identifying specific behaviors that need to be changed. Behaviors can be negative behaviors that need to be decreased (e.g., inappropriately getting out of seat, interrupting while parent is on the telephone) or positive behaviors that need to be increased (e.g., raising hand, waiting to ask a question).

The Pinpointing Form provides assistance in problem identification by focusing on observable behaviors or actions. Typically, efforts to intervene focus on decreasing negative behaviors and first involve the use of punishment procedures. This form also permits identification of adaptive behaviors, thus helping direct attention toward more positive interventions as a starting point.

Pinpointing Form

Child's name _____ Date _____

Form completed by _____

Please identify negative behaviors (behaviors to decrease) and positive behaviors (behaviors to increase).

Behaviors to decrease

1. _____

   _____

   _____

2. _____

   _____

   _____

3. _____

   _____

   _____

4. _____

   _____

   _____

5. _____

   _____

   _____

Behaviors to increase

1. _____

   _____

   _____

2. _____

   _____

   _____

3. _____

   _____

   _____

4. _____

   _____

   _____

5. _____

   _____

   _____

From *The Behavior Problems Resource Kit,* © 2010 by Michael J. Asher, Steven B. Gordon, Michael C. Selbst, and Mark Cooperberg, Champaign, IL: Research Press (800-519-2707, www.researchpress.com)

PART 2

MEASUREMENT AND FUNCTIONAL BEHAVIORAL ASSESSMENT

After a student's problem is identified, there are many questions to be answered. For example: How often does the behavior occur? When does it occur? What happens next? Why is this happening? Part 2 contains forms that measure and assess the frequency, rate, duration, and intensity of the child's problem behaviors.

Measuring the problem behaviors allows for an appraisal of the severity of the problem so that there is justification for putting effort into intervention. Measurement also establishes a frame of reference by which to evaluate the effectiveness of interventions. The term baseline refers to the current level of the problem behavior and can be expressed in the following ways:

- frequency (e.g., 8 hits)
- rate (e.g., 1.2 call-outs per minute)
- percent of occurrence (e.g., 23 percent of the observed intervals)
- duration (e.g., 17 minutes to complete the assignment)
- intensity (e.g., 4 on a 5-point scale of angry outburst)

Measurement across settings such as classroom, playground, home, and after-school allows patterns to be identified which will facilitate interventions directed toward the most problematic setting.

There is an advantage to having a variety of individuals in the child's life complete measurement questionnaires. A child's mother, father, and teacher(s) may each provide significant information related to possible controlling variables.

Functional behavioral assessment is the gold standard when problem behaviors don't respond to standard interventions (such as posting written rules in a classroom). The Individuals with Disabilities Education Act (2004) explains that an FBA is required when a child's behavior interferes with the child's learning or the learning of others.

An FBA builds on the material presented in Part 1 by identifying the events that precede and follow the problem behavior (antecedents and consequences). The goal is to arrive at a descriptive summary of the problem behavior and a hypothesis as to the function or purpose of the problem behavior.

Forms and procedures in this section contain critical questions to help clinicians, school personnel, and parents develop hypotheses about what may be motivating the child to engage in the problem behaviors. These hypotheses may include factors related to the child's motivation to:

- gain attention from adults or peers
- escape or avoid a demand, request, or social situation
- gain access to something preferred (or tangible)
- obtain or avoid something that is internally or automatically reinforcing (e.g., increase listening to pleasant music, decrease painful headache)

The forms and procedures in this section also prompt the adult (parent, school personnel) to consider prior and current interventions, and the child's response to these interventions.

Specifically included here are the following:

- School Antecedent-Behavior-Consequence (ABC) Recording (p. 47)
    School ABC Recording Form
- Interval Recording (p. 54)
    Interval Recording Form
- Functional Behavioral Assessment (p. 56)
    Functional Behavioral Assessment Scale
    Functional Behavioral Assessment Scale Scoring Form
    Functional Behavioral Assessment Classroom Checklist
- Scatter Plot (p. 64)
    Sample Scatter Plot Form
    Scatter Plot Form

School Antecedent-Behavior-Consequence (ABC) Recording

Indirect methods of functional behavior assessment (FBA) involve interviews and questionnaires, but direct methods provide formal observations of the child in naturalistic settings where the behavior occurs.

The School ABC Recording Form provides the observer with a tool to organize the observations of the child's problem behaviors, to analyze them, and finally to create hypotheses about the functions of the behaviors. This information can be linked to a behavior intervention plan (BIP).

The triggering event is the occurrence of the target behavior (TB) and is anecdotally noted in the Behavior column of the form. For example "hits peer" or "throws object". These target behaviors may be determined in advance of the formal observation by way of the interview, questionnaires and/or record review.

When the target behavior occurs, the observer makes an entry in the Behavior column. Then, the observer enters anecdotal information in the following columns:

- time and initials of observer (to account for the possibility that multiple observers may be involved with data collection)
- location
- activity
- antecedent
- behavior
- consequence
- outcome

Because the School ABC Recording Form provides an organized table for entering observed information, it frees the observer from writing lengthy anecdotal records that detract from the formal observation.

- The entries in Table 1 provide examples of locations, activities, behaviors, consequences, and outcomes that might be included in a School ABC Recording Form.

- Table 2 shows a portion of a one-day observation of Robert, a nine-year-old student whose challenging behaviors were observed in language arts class and confirmed as typical by Robert's teacher.

- After recording the data, the observer converted each anecdotal record into a numerical value on a spreadsheet, as shown in Table 3. The classroom location was assigned a value of 1. With regard to activity, independent seatwork was assigned a value of 1, peer cooperative learning group was assigned a value of 3, and transition was assigned a numerical value of 7. (Numerical values were assigned by the observer after the observation for data analysis, using a pivot table format in Excel.) Each row represents one occurrence of a significant problem behavior, with each number representing its associated variables.

- The graphs shown in Figures 1 through 6 illustrate how the data collected using the School ABC Recording Form can be represented to promote better understanding of Robert's challenging behavior.

Table 1

Possible Entries on ABC Recording Form

Location	Activity	Antecedent	Behavior	Consequence	Outcome
Classroom	Independent work	Instruction to group	Noncomply	Verbal redirection	CB stopped
Hallway	Group work	Instruction to child	Verbally noisy	Reprimand	CB continued
Cafeteria	Free time	Peer initiates interaction	Destroys property	Ignore	CB increased

Table 2

Sample ABC Recording Form for Robert

Student's name ___Robert_____ Date __May 6_____

Completed by ___RG (teacher)_____

Date	Time/Initials	Location	Activity	Antecedent	Behavior	Consequence	Outcome
May 6	9:01 a.m./RG	class	workbook	write name	whines	ignore	stopped
	9:08 a.m./RG	class	workbook	write name	yells	verbal redirection	stopped
	9:15 a.m./RG	class	free play	clean up command	throws object	restraint	stopped
	9:21 a.m./RG	class	snack	teacher asks question	yells	ignore	stopped

Table 3

ABC Data for Robert

Event	Location	Activity	Antecedent	Behavior	Consequence	Outcome
1	1	7	10	5	4	1
2	1	3	6	6	1	2
3	1	3	1	6	1	2
4	1	3	1	6	1	2
5	1	3	1	6	1	2
6	1	1	1	6	1	1
7	1	1	1	7	1	2

Figure 1
Types of Challenging Behaviors Displayed by Robert

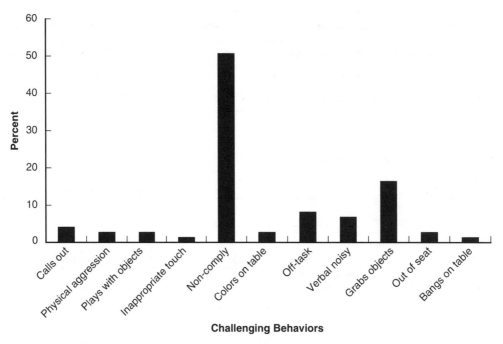

Challenging Behaviors

Figure 2
Locations of Challenging Behaviors Displayed by Robert

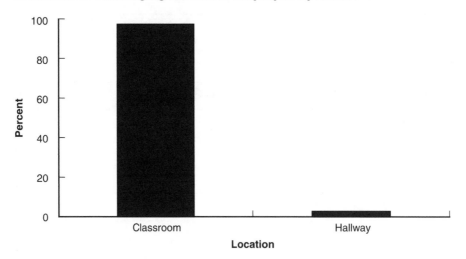

Location

Figure 3
Activities in Which Robert Displays Challenging Behaviors

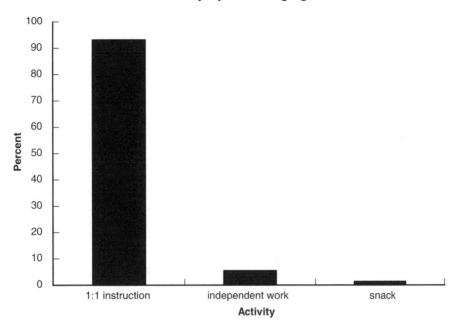

Figure 4
Antecedent Events After Which Robert Displays Challenging Behaviors

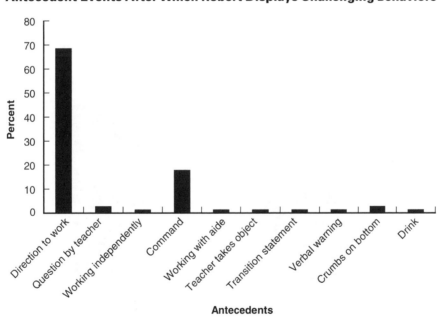

Figure 5

**Consequences Robert Receives Following the Occurence
of Challanging Behaviors**

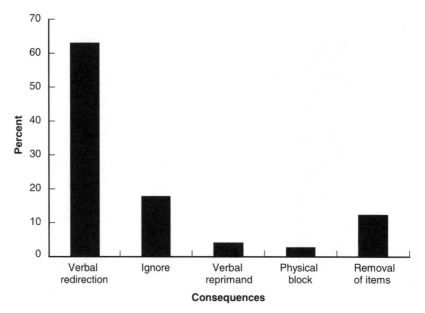

Figure 6

Outcome of Consequences for Robert's Challenging Behaviors

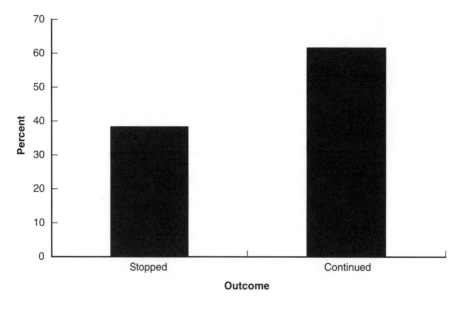

As soon as the target behavior occurs, enter a word that best describes it. Then briefly and quickly complete an entry in each of the adjoining cells in the row. Continue until the observation is complete.

Student's name _____ Date _____

Form completed by _____

Date	Time/Initials	Location	Activity	Antecedent	Behavior	Consequence	Outcome

From *The Behavior Problems Resource Kit,* © 2010 by Michael J. Asher, Steven B. Gordon, Michael C. Selbst, and Mark Cooperberg, Champaign, IL: Research Press (800-519-2707, www.researchpress.com)

Interval Recording

Interval recording is a versatile method to record ongoing behavior or discrete occurrences of behaviors. For example, interval recording could be used to collect data on self-initiated social interactions during a 20-minute free play situation. The observer would divide the 20 minutes into equal intervals of a predetermined unit of time (e.g., 15 seconds).

Partial interval recording requires the observer to note whether or not the target behavior, in this case self-initiated social interactions, occurred at all during the interval. Whether the target behavior occurred one time or twenty times, the observer simply notes that it occurred.

Whole interval recording requires the target behavior to occur for the entire interval for it to be recorded. For example, if the target behavior was task engagement (defined as eyes on speaker, writing relevant answers, following all classroom rules), the observer records its occurrence if it occurred for the entire length of the interval.

A variant of interval recording is *time sampling,* where the observer notes whether or not the target behavior is occurring at the end of the interval. For example, if a 30-minute block of time is chosen for observation, then the time could be divided into 30 one-minute intervals and the observer would note whether or not the target behavior occurs at the end of each minute. The demands on the observer are minimal because time sampling requires looking at the child for only one second and making a recording ("yes" or "no").

Data from partial or whole interval recording or time sampling is reported as a percentage derived by dividing the total number of intervals into the number of intervals in which the behavior occurred multiplied by 100 (e.g., $20/40 \times 100 = 50$ percent).

It is recommended that data be collected on a typically developing same gender peer as a normative frame of reference. Procedurally, it is best for the observer to use one interval for the identified child, followed by using the next interval for the peer, then the next interval for the identified child, and so forth, which controls for time and activity. The Interval Recording Form on the following page permits entries for both children.

Interval Recording Form

Circle the type of interval recording and indicate the length of the interval.
Begin with the target child and alternate with a typical peer of the same gender.

Child's name _____ Date _____

Form completed by _____

Target behavior _____

Interval recording: whole   partial   interval   Duration: _____

Student								
Peer								

Student								
Peer								

Student								
Peer								

Student								
Peer								

Student								
Peer								

Student								
Peer								

Student								
Peer								

Student								
Peer								

Student								
Peer								

Functional Behavioral Assessment

The Functional Behavioral Assessment Scale (FBAS) assesses the function or motivation of a child's behavior. There are three forms included in this section:

- Functional Behavioral Assessment Scale Form
- Functional Behavioral Assessment Scale Scoring Form
- Functional Behavioral Assessment Scale Classroom Checklist

A functional behavioral assessment determines what is motivating the child's behavior. It is recognized in the field of behavior psychology that all behavior is motivated by specific functions. This knowledge is essential for both targeting interventions and identifying appropriate reinforcement; without this information, interventions may fail and reinforcement of undesirable behavior may occur.

There are many specific functions, or motivating factors, for the problem behavior. The Functional Behavioral Assessment Scale includes eight variables (four categories of variables, each with two types).

The *escape variable* assesses:

- escaping or avoiding tasks and environmental demands (e.g., avoiding or prolonging class work or homework)
- escaping or avoiding an unpleasant social situation

The *attention variable* identifies the target behavior as a means of drawing attention to one's self (e.g., the class clown). The attention variable assesses:

- adult attention
- peer attention

The *tangible reward variable* assesses tangible consequences of behaviors that are used to obtain a desired object or activities in the child's environment (e.g., tantrum when denied a desired object). The tangible reward variable assesses:

- tangible object
- tangible activity

The *automatic/sensory stimulation variable* assesses the sensory needs of the individual (e.g., increased physical movement during paper-and-pencil tasks or increased stimulation when a task is uninteresting). A behavior may have more than one function or motivation. Therefore, it is possible to check more than one category. The automatic/sensory stimulation variable assesses:

- automatic positive reinforcement
- automatic negative reinforcement

The Functional Behavioral Assessment Scale Scoring Form allows the clinician to gather the data from the FBAS form and use results to target appropriate interventions and reinforcements.

The Functional Behavioral Assessment Scale Classroom Checklist identifies significant classroom variables, such as the demographics of the classroom, classroom physical environment, teacher's instructional style, and classroom materials.

Functional Behavioral Assessment Scale

Child's name _____ Date _____

Form completed by _____

Directions

1. Enter a specific target behavior (e.g., she argues with others) rather than a more general description of the individual's behavior (e.g., he gets upset). Behavior should be described in measurable terms (an operational definition) so that others could clearly identify when it occurs.

2. Specify the situation where the target behavior is a problem (e.g., at home after dinner, during a classroom activity, lunch, during one-on-one teaching, in math class, etc.).

3. Rate each of the 24 items by circling the number that corresponds to how often the child engages in the behavior indicated within the identified setting.

Target behavior _____

_____

Operational definition _____

_____

_____

Specific setting in which the target behavior may occur _____

_____

_____

From *The Behavior Problems Resource Kit,* © 2010 by Michael J. Asher, Steven B. Gordon, Michael C. Selbst, and Mark Cooperberg, Champaign, IL: Research Press (800-519-2707, www.researchpress.com)

Does the behavior occur . . .	Never 0	Rarely 1	Sometimes 2	Often 3	Almost always 4
Escape and/or Avoid Task					
1. When the child perceives a task as too boring?	0	1	2	3	4
2. When the child perceives a task as too challenging or difficult?	0	1	2	3	4
3. When the child perceives a task as too long?	0	1	2	3	4
Escape and/or Avoid Social Situation					
4. When the child has to do academic work with other students?	0	1	2	3	4
5. When the child needs to present (e.g., make a speech, play an instrument, etc.) in front of others?	0	1	2	3	4
6. When the child enters a group of students who are playing?	0	1	2	3	4
Adult Attention					
7. When the child is trying to get an adult to look at, talk with, play with, or spend time with him/her?	0	1	2	3	4
8. When an adult has stopped looking at, talking with, playing with, or spending time with him/her?	0	1	2	3	4
9. When the adult is interacting with another child or adult?	0	1	2	3	4
Peer Attention					
10. When the child is trying to get another child to look at, talk with, play with, or spend time with him/her?	0	1	2	3	4
11. When a child has stopped looking at, talking with, playing with, or spending time with him/her?	0	1	2	3	4
12. When a specific child with whom he/she wants to interact has been interacting with another child or adult?	0	1	2	3	4
Tangible Object					
13. When the child is trying gain access to a preferred object (e.g., toy, game)?	0	1	2	3	4
14. When a preferred object has been withdrawn or removed from the child?	0	1	2	3	4
15. When an object is not working properly?	0	1	2	3	4

Functional Behavioral Assessment Scale (page 2 of 3)

Does the behavior occur . . .	Never 0	Rarely 1	Sometimes 2	Often 3	Almost always 4
Tangible Activity					
16. When the child is trying to gain access to a preferred activity (e.g., using a computer, playing sports, watching television, going to the mall)?	0	1	2	3	4
17. When a preferred activity has ended or been removed (e.g., recess, television show ends, privilege removed)?	0	1	2	3	4
18. When a specific activity is not going as expected or planned?	0	1	2	3	4
Automatic Positive Reinforcement					
19. When the child is engaged in a pleasant activity?	0	1	2	3	4
20. When the child has no demands placed on him/her?	0	1	2	3	4
21. Frequently or continuously, even if there is no one else present?	0	1	2	3	4
Automatic Negative Reinforcement					
22. When the child is experiencing some physical discomfort (e.g., headache, stomachache, sore muscles)?	0	1	2	3	4
23. When there is a loud noise present in the environment (e.g., screaming or crying)?	0	1	2	3	4
24. When the stimuli in the environment are significantly different than normal (e.g., change in temperature, lighting, seating arrangement)?	0	1	2	3	4

Score the Functional Behavioral Assessment Scale by adding the items from each functional domain (e.g., adult attention). Each total is then divided by the number of items (e.g., 3). Finally, sort the domains by the highest mean score so that the domain with the highest mean score is ranked "1" and the domain with the lowest mean score is ranked "8."

Escape and/or avoid task

Total of items 1, 2, 3 _____   Mean score _____   Rank order (1–8) _____

Escape and/or avoid social situation

Total of items 4, 5, 6 _____   Mean score _____   Rank order (1–8) _____

Adult attention

Total of items 7, 8, 9 _____   Mean score _____   Rank order (1–8) _____

Peer attention

Total of items 10, 11, 12 _____   Mean score _____   Rank order (1–8) _____

Tangible object

Total of items 13, 14, 15 _____   Mean score _____   Rank order (1–8) _____

Tangible activity

Total of items 16, 17, 18 _____   Mean score _____   Rank order (1–8) _____

Automatic positive reinforcement

Total of items 19, 20, 21 _____   Mean score _____   Rank order (1–8) _____

Automatic negative reinforcement

Total of items 22, 23, 24 _____   Mean score _____   Rank order (1–8) _____

Functional Behavioral Assessment Classroom Checklist

Child's name _____ Date _____

Form completed by _____

Demographics of Classroom	Response	Comments
1. number of students present		
2. number of male students present		
3. number of female students present		
4. staff members present		
Classroom Physical Environment		
1. adequate lighting	Yes / No	
2. adequate noise level	Yes / No	
3. tile floor	Yes / No	
4. some carpet area	Yes / No	
5. row and column seating	Yes / No	
6. desks grouped in pods	Yes / No	
Teacher's Instructional Style		
1. Voice inflection and tone were positive	Yes / No	
2. More positive than negative comments	Yes / No	
3. Made eye contact with students	Yes / No	
4. Lecture style	Yes / No	
5. Visual stimuli incorporated	Yes / No	
6. Hands-on activities incorporated	Yes / No	
7. Small-group activities incorporated	Yes / No	
8. Warnings given prior to transitions	Yes / No	
9. Directions contain adequate number of steps and are not complex	Yes / No	

From *The Behavior Problems Resource Kit,* © 2010 by Michael J. Asher, Steven B. Gordon, Michael C. Selbst, and Mark Cooperberg, Champaign, IL: Research Press (800-519-2707, www.researchpress.com)

Classroom Materials		
1. Behavior rules posted	Yes / No	
2. Rules stated positively, if posted	Yes / No	
3. Classroom schedule posted	Yes / No	
4. Age appropriate toys and games	Yes / No	
5. Age appropriate books	Yes / No	

Scatter Plot

The Scatter Plot method of data collection is used during baseline or when intervention begins, but it is not a substitute for a functional behavior assessment. The Scatter Plot Form records the occurrence of the target behavior only during specific time periods, such as periods in the day based on academic subjects (e.g., math, language arts, etc.) or activities (e.g., breakfast, dinner, etc.).

An inspection of the data indicates the times of day or the activities associated with higher and lower rates of the target behavior. This provides greater precision in designing interventions. The Scatter Plot Form was used with Monique, a second-grade student who had difficulty remaining seated during the school day. The Sample Scatter Plot Form, completed for one day, indicates that Monique was out of her seat a total of 13 times, all during academic instruction. The highest recorded frequency was math (5), and the lowest was social studies (2). These data would contribute to developing a better understanding of the function that "out of seat" serves and to the development of an effective behavior intervention plan for Monique.

Sample Scatter Plot Form

Child's name ___Monique___ Date ___February 16___

Target behavior ___Out of seat___

Definition ___Removing herself from assigned area for 30 seconds or more___

Form completed by ___Ms. McMahon___

Period/Activity	Occurrences	Total
1. Reading	III	3
2. Physical education		
3. Lunch		
4. Math	ﬀﬀ	5
5. Art		
6. Language Arts	III	3
7. Social Studies	II	2
8.		
		Total for day ___13___

Scatter Plot Form

Child's name _____ Date _____

Target behavior _____

Definition _____

Form completed by _____

Period/Activity	Occurrences	Total
1.		
2.		
3.		
4.		
5.		
6.		
7.		
8.		
		Total for day _____

From *The Behavior Problems Resource Kit,* © 2010 by Michael J. Asher, Steven B. Gordon, Michael C. Selbst, and Mark Cooperberg, Champaign, IL: Research Press (800-519-2707, www.researchpress.com)

PART 3

INTERVENTIONS

Many intervention strategies look good on paper, but they often fail because of issues that haven't been directly addressed. These issues include problem identification, measurement, and functional assessment. The psychological difficulties children experience must be recognized as real difficulties that interfere with appropriate development. The disorders addressed in this book are disabling conditions just as physical or sensory impairments are disabling. This section offers evidence-based interventions with reproducible forms to be used with all childhood disorders.

Much of the behavior management material available for parents, teachers, and mental health providers is organized by specific problem (e.g., noncompliance, work refusal, anxiety). These "cookbook approaches" offer many possible solutions, but they tend to view the adult as a technician who applies methods without understanding the motivation or function behind the specific behavior.

Parents and professionals today are much more than technicians. They understand the nature of the child's problems, analyze the problems carefully, select an appropriate target behavior for intervention, and define and measure the target behavior. This allows parents and professionals to systematically intervene with an approach logically connected to the function of the target behavior, and then to evaluate the effectiveness of the intervention. If the clinician, teacher, or parent is not involved at this level, the intervention has little chance of success.

The procedures and forms included here are divided into three sections: Behavior and Social Skill Intervention Plans, Antecedent Interventions, and Consequence Interventions.

BEHAVIOR AND SOCIAL SKILLS INTERVENTION PLANS

As described in Part 2, functional behavioral assessments pinpoint problem behaviors, identify the triggers for these problem behaviors, and clarify the child's motivation for the behaviors. It is important to remember that all functions of behavior should be understood as the child's attempt to communicate needs. With this information in hand, clinicians, school personnel, and parents can address classroom modifications and accommodations that are most likely to support the child. Two forms assist in this process: the Behavior Intervention Plan Form and the Social Skills Intervention Plan Form.

ANTECEDENT INTERVENTIONS: ALTERING THE ENVIRONMENT

Antecedent interventions involve attempts to alter the environment for children and adolescents so that desirable, prosocial behaviors are more likely to occur and undesirable behaviors are less likely to occur. Efforts are proactive, directed toward change *before* the problem presents itself. By being preventive in nature, antecedent interventions avoid the common overuse of consequence interventions (e.g., sticker charts posted on refrigerators and taped to desks).

Accommodations related to environmental structure, organization of space, establishing roles for others, establishing rules, managing time, materials and resources can significantly affect children's success. By considering the strategies and issues described in this section, parents and clinicians will be better able to minimize the chance that a problem will occur and prevent the small problem from growing into a larger one.

Antecedent interventions have perhaps the greatest impact on children experiencing psychological problems, but they have the potential to benefit all children, not just children with behavior problems. As such, these interventions should be in the repertoires of all who support a child's success. Included in this section are the Educational Accommodation Plan Form and a number of Coaching for Change procedures and forms.

For a complete list of procedures and forms included in this section, see page 86.

BEHAVIORAL INTERVENTIONS: TEACHING REPLACEMENT BEHAVIORS

The goal of the interventions in this section is to teach behaviors to help children and adolescents overcome emotional, social, and behavioral deficits. The objectives are to improve the child's ability to make and keep friends, express themselves appropriately, solve problems, manage frustration, develop more self-confidence, and behave more appropriately. Efforts are directed towards teaching specific replacement behaviors and skills to help the child adapt to situational demands. The emphasis is on developing an awareness of the problem and outlining and training the child to use the steps to overcome the obstacles preventing success.

The forms and procedures in this section will help children understand their difficulties and examine the cognitive course of their problems. New behaviors are broken down into steps that can be practiced. Role play becomes an important part of the reciprocal interaction between adult and child that provides the child with the opportunity to practice the skills. For transfer and generalization it is essential to practice these new behaviors and strategies in multiple settings, with different people and differing examples.

These interventions are useful to expand the behavioral repertoires of all children. Through the use of the strategies described in this section, teachers, parents, and clinicians will maximize the chances that children with functional deficits will grow and become successful. The procedures and forms included in this section include Feelings Management, the 3-D Skills Approach, and Cue and Review, among others.

For a complete list of procedures and forms in this section, see page 116.

CONSEQUENCE INTERVENTIONS: CONTROLLING POSITIVE AND NEGATIVE REINFORCEMENT

Consequence interventions modify behavior through the application of positive or negative consequences and are perhaps the oldest and most commonly used interventions in homes and classrooms. Positive consequences increase the frequency, intensity and/or duration of a given behavior, whereas negative consequences decrease a behavior's frequency, intensity and/or duration.

Consequence interventions are effective for almost all children experiencing psychological problems. However, specific guidelines for their design and use are important: First, understand the cause and nature of the child's disorder and avoid misconceptions and judgmental thinking about the child's specific problem. Second, give careful consideration to the child's developmental level or developmental delays. In order for interventions to be successful, parents, teachers and clinicians must recognize the limitations of cognitive, social and emotional development. Third, before using a consequence intervention, structure the environment by employing appropriate antecedent interventions. Finally, any consequence intervention must be understood in relationship to the child's functional behavioral assessment, or the specific motivations driving the child's behavior.

As with all consequence interventions, it is also important to determine that the child is motivated by the reinforcers chosen and to ensure that consequences delivered are not actually reinforcing the target behavior. Appendix A provides reinforcement inventories for children and adolescents.

Some of the procedures and forms included in this section are the Behavior Contract and Scorecard and the School and Home Environment Learning Programs.

For a complete list of procedures and forms in this section, see page 158.

BEHAVIOR AND SOCIAL SKILLS INTERVENTION PLANS

BEHAVIOR INTERVENTION PLAN

The functional behavioral assessments conducted in Part 2 are necessary to move to the next step in the process—development of a behavior intervention plan. The Behavior Intervention Plan (BIP) Form guides the step-by-step process that includes positive behavior supports such as classroom modifications and accommodations required to address the behaviors of concern and to provide the child with replacement behaviors (i.e., new skills). The Behavior Intervention Plan Checklist is designed to help ensure that the plan is complete. Two sample Behavior Intervention Plans are included in Appendix B.

SOCIAL SKILLS INTERVENTION PLAN

The Social Skills Intervention Plan (SSIP) Form provides a framework from which to develop a plan to improve a child's social skills. This form is similar to the BIP in many ways, but the SSIP is specific to social skills interventions. Various skills can be included in an SSIP Form, including feelings identification, feelings expression, reading nonverbal cues, conversational skills, game-playing skills, and so forth.

The form outlines the specific deficit in social behavior, including means of assessment, identified deficits, and information about the deficit (frequency, location, antecedents, and consequences). The next step provides clinically useful information about how the deficit impacts the child's functioning at school, with family, in relationships, and in the child's self-esteem.

The clinician then identifies possible functions of the child's behavior, as well as the results of any previous interventions. The form includes a section to outline the specific skill that will be taught, including the positive behavior supports used to develop and strengthen the skill. The actual intervention is outlined in a manner that permits data collection and monitoring. The clinician is able to set priorities for which skills need to be addressed so that multiple skills can be addressed sequentially. A crucial aspect of social skills training is generalization, so an emphasis on communication and parent involvement is built into the form. Two sample Social Skills Intervention Plans are also included in Appendix B.

Please use additional pages if necessary.

Child's name _____ Date _____

Age _____ Grade _____

Form completed by _____

1. **Describe the target behavior (the behavior to be reduced) in sufficient detail so two independent observers could understand it.**

2. **Describe baseline results, or the current level of behavior, including dates data were collected, frequency, duration, range of frequency, and/or intensity.**

3. **List circumstances under which the target behavior occurs or does not occur.**

4. List prior interventions (if any) and the effectiveness of these interventions.

5. Place a checkmark next to and explain probable function(s) of the behavior. All functions of behavior should be understood as the child's attempt to communicate his or her needs.

☐ Escape and/or avoid task

☐ Escape and/or avoid social situation

☐ Adult attention

☐ Peer attention

☐ Tangible object

☐ Tangible activity

☐ Automatic positive reinforcement (seeks to initiate or continue pleasurable sensory stimulation)

☐ Automatic negative reinforcement (seeks to reduce or eliminate uncomfortable sensory stimulation)

Behavior Intervention Plan Form (page 2 of 6)

6. Identify and list "replacement behaviors" to be developed and reinforced to replace negative/target behaviors. (Replacement behaviors are the prosocial or appropriate behaviors that will help the child communicate wants or needs.)

7. Describe positive supports/ interventions to develop or strengthen replacement behaviors.

8. Identify the reinforcement schedule (e.g., fixed or variable interval or fixed or variable ratio schedule).

9. Specify the procedures to implement when the target behavior occurs (e.g., planned ignoring, Sit and Think, verbal or physical prompt, correction procedure).

10. List materials required (e.g., timer, counter, data sheets, token board, picture symbols).

11. List the environmental changes/classroom modifications (e.g., preferential seating, lighting, calm area, sound amplification, type of desk/chair).

12. Describe data collection and management system (e.g., event recording, duration recording, time sampling, interval recording, permanent product, intensity rating, anecdotal recording).

13. Describe conditions under which the supports/interventions will be implemented.

14. Describe conditions under which the supports/interventions will be terminated.

15. **Describe the plan for parent involvement (e.g., sharing data summary, generalization strategies, parent data collection or reinforcement, information exchange between school and home).**

16. **Provide the frequency of review.**

17. **Is informed consent required?** ☐ Yes ☐ No

Date of implementation _____ Baseline rate _____

Date of review _____ Baseline rate _____

Date of termination _____ Baseline rate _____

Behavior Intervention Plan Checklist

Please use the following checklist as a guide to facilitate the design of an effective, comprehensive behavior intervention plan.

	Yes	No
1. Has a target behavior been clearly defined so that two independent observers could agree?	☐	☐
2. Has a functional analysis been completed?	☐	☐
3. Has a measurement procedure been selected?	☐	☐
4. Has a period of time for data collection been chosen?	☐	☐
5. Has a person been identified to collect the data?	☐	☐
6. Does the intervention identify a positive target behavior to strengthen (i.e., replacement behaviors)?	☐	☐
7. Has a reinforcement survey been completed?	☐	☐
8. Does the intervention include an attempt to increase a replacement behavior by using positive reinforcement?	☐	☐
9. Has a reinforcement schedule been developed?	☐	☐
10. Does the intervention address antecedent modification?	☐	☐
11. If a punishment procedure is used, are there appropriate safeguards?	☐	☐
12. Have staff members associated themselves with reinforcers to become reinforcing themselves to students (i.e., pairing)?	☐	☐
13. Is a total communication approach used to increase functional communication (e.g., language, PECS, sign, gestures)?	☐	☐
14. Is there a multisensory, hands-on learning environment, emphasizing engaging tasks and task choices?	☐	☐

Signatures

Parent _____ Date _____

Parent _____ Date _____

Teacher _____ Date _____

Teacher _____ Date _____

Case manager _____ Date _____

Behavioral consultant _____ Date _____

Administrator _____ Date _____

Other _____ Date _____

Other _____ Date _____

Please use additional pages if necessary.

Child's name _____ Date _____

Age _____ Grade _____

Form completed by _____

1. Identify the specific deficit in social behavior.

  a. What is the means of assessment (e.g., social skills rating scale, observation, etc.)?

  b. What are the identified deficits in social skills (e.g., conversational skills, empathy, anger management, interpersonal problem solving)?

  c. What is the estimated frequency of the social skill deficit? (How often is the deficit displayed?)

  d. Where does the skill deficit occur (e.g., classroom, playground, lunch room, in the community, at home)?

e. With whom does the skill deficit occur (e.g., same-aged peers, older children, younger children, adults)?

f. What are the antecedents, the circumstances that set the occasion for the skill deficit to occur?

g. What circumstances rarely set the occasion for the skill deficit to occur?

h. What are the consequences (circumstances that follow the occurrence of the skill deficit)?

2. What is the impact of the skill deficit on the following?

a. school performance

b. family interactions

c. student's relationship with peers

d. student's self-esteem/confidence

3. **What are the hypothesized function(s) of the skill deficit? All functions of behavior should be understood as the child's attempt to communicate his or her needs.**

☐ Escape and/or avoid task

☐ Escape and/or avoid social situation

☐ Adult attention

☐ Peer attention

☐ Tangible object

☐ Tangible activity

☐ Automatic positive reinforcement

☐ Automatic negative reinforcement

4. **Describe any previous interventions to address social problems and their results.**

5. **Identify the social skill(s) to be taught.**

6. **Describe the positive behavior supports/interventions to develop or strengthen the identified skill. Describe settings (where?), personnel (who?), examples (what?), and modality (how?).**

7. What interventions will be used when the skill deficit occurs?

8. Describe the data collection and management system.

9. List the personnel responsible for each aspect of intervention (i.e., training and practice).

10. What is the skill priority list? Please be specific.

11. What are the conditions (i.e., criteria) under which the next skill will be introduced?

12. Describe the role of parent involvement (e.g., frequency of communication, method of communication, implementation of interventions).

13. What is the consultation and review procedure (weekly, bimonthly, monthly, other)?

Date of implementation _____   Baseline rate _____

Date of review _____   Baseline rate _____

Date of termination _____   Baseline rate _____

ANTECEDENT INTERVENTIONS: ALTERING THE ENVIRONMENT

COACHING FOR CHANGE PROCEDURES AND FORMS

Coaching is an essential part of programming for a child or adolescent who has difficulties in structured and unstructured settings. The coaching procedures and forms in this section help with relationships, rules, consequences, and particular problem situations. Because children with behavioral issues often have trouble with rule-governed behavior, extensive procedures for rule violation are included. To ensure maximum effectiveness, several of the rule violation procedures include forms to help the respondent monitor use of the procedure.

Coaching for Change procedures and forms include the following:

- Relationship Enhancement Form (p. 89)
- Plan Ahead Form (p. 90)
- Social Buddy Form (p. 91)
- Frequent Feedback Procedure (p. 92)
    Frequent Feedback Form
- Rule Establishment Procedure (p. 94)
    Rule Establishment Form
- Rule Review Procedure (p. 97)
    Rule Review Monitoring Form
- Rule Evaluation Procedure (p. 99)
    Rule Evaluation Form
- Rule Compliance Procedure (p. 101)
    Rule Compliance Form
- Rule Violation Procedures (p. 103)
    Rule Violation Monitoring Form–School
    Rule Violation Monitoring Form–Home

EDUCATIONAL ACCOMMODATIONS

Students with disabling conditions who have substantial limitations in the educational setting are eligible for educational accommodations under Section 504 of the Rehabilitation Act of 1973. This act, which prohibits discrimination against an individual with a disability in any program that receives federal financial assistance, defines a person with a disability as anyone who has a mental or physical impairment that substantially limits one or more major life activities, including self-care, performing manual tasks, walking, seeing, hearing, speaking, breathing, learning, and working. There needs to be documentation regarding the student having such impairments to establish the need for accommodation.

In order to fulfill their obligation under Section 504, school districts must recognize their responsibility to avoid discrimination in any policy or practice regarding their students. School districts therefore have the added responsibility to identify, evaluate, and determine whether a child is eligible under Section 504, as well as to afford access to a free and appropriate education and any necessary services.

Educational accommodation plans are designed to provide parents, teachers, school administrators, and students the opportunity to consider potential educational accommodations in physical aspects of the classroom, lesson presentation, assignments, test taking, behavior/discipline, and other areas (e.g., medication, counseling, social skills training). Accomodations provide different ways for students to receive classroom information and then communicate their knowledge. Whether through Section 504 or an Individualized Education Program (IEP) plans, accomodations can be formal additions to the educational landscape for a student with a disabling condition. Accomodations are adjustments to instruction to make sure a student has equal access to the educational, social and behavioral curriculum, with a focus on success. Accommodations provide classroom teachers with a topography of student needs to guide classroom instruction, testing, and social and behavioral success. Accomodations are generally in students' IEPs, although they are not specifically required. The content provided in this section can allow classroom teachers a means to help students with difficulties meet the same standards set for all students.

Some general education teachers, with or without the support of the school intervention and referral services committee (student support team, pupil assistance committee) agree informally to make accomodations in their classrooms for students with difficulties. Whether formally or informally, accomodation plans need to be assessed for the student's response to intervention and continued needs. If used, plans must evolve and not remain in place as a means of decreased expectations. Parents and school personnel need to play an active role in teaching skills that can increase the student's abilities and allow decreasing accommodation use. In some cases, supportive accomodations may need to continue to provide equal access to educational and posteducational environments.

The Educational Accommodation Plan Form (on p. 108) lists a number of common accommodations in the general education classroom in various categories.

Relationship Enhancement Form

It is useful to develop a special relationship between a supervising adult and a child with any behavioral difficulties. This form helps establish that the adult is there to assist or help in any way possible.

Child's name _____ Date _____

Form completed by _____

1. Talk to the child about interests (e.g., sports, skateboarding, videogaming, etc.) at a time free from crisis. Listen carefully and in a nonjudgmental manner. List at least three of the child's interests below. This should not be a singular event—instead, aim for five minutes once every other week.

   Interest 1. _____

   Interest 2. _____

   Interest 3. _____

2. Find out two areas of interest that you have in common with the child and list below.

   Interest 1. _____

   Interest 2. _____

3. What does this child know about you? Give him/her time to ask you questions. Below, describe what you told about yourself.

   _____

   _____

4. Identify a time and place to talk regularly with the child about the child's interests and the interests you have in common. Set a date with the child and keep a record of the information you learn.

   Time _____   Place _____

The Plan Ahead Procedure consists of reviewing in advance any obstacles the child or adolescent might encounter (e.g., being teased or rejected). This process helps the child to develop alternative solutions if these obstacles develop.

Child's name _____ Date _____

Form completed by _____

1. List three triggers/situations that cause problems for this child.

   _____

   _____

   _____

2. List three alternative solutions to overcome these obstacles.

   _____

   _____

   _____

3. List three ways you will help prevent recurrent problems this child experiences.

   _____

   _____

   _____

The Social Buddy Procedure helps identify in advance a peer or group of peers who can provide assistance to the child during high-risk situations. These children can prompt and reinforce appropriate behavior during these times. Attention must be paid to the careful selection and training of social buddies.

Child's name _____ Date _____

Form completed by _____

Which children have been identified to serve as social buddies?

1. _____
2. _____
3. _____

What prompts or cues will the social buddies use to initiate appropriate behavior?

1. _____
2. _____
3. _____

What types of reinforcing comments will the social buddies use when the child displays appropriate behavior?

1. _____
2. _____
3. _____

What activities have been negotiated for the social buddy and the child to participate in together?

1. _____
2. _____
3. _____

What form of training will take place to maintain the Social Buddy Procedure?

1. _____
2. _____
3. _____

Daily meetings (time/place)_____

Weekly meetings (time/place) _____

From *The Behavior Problems Resource Kit,* © 2010 by Michael J. Asher, Steven B. Gordon, Michael C. Selbst, and Mark Cooperberg, Champaign, IL: Research Press (800-519-2707, www.researchpress.com)

Frequent Feedback Procedure

Children and adolescents with behavioral and functional difficulties often have a greater need for feedback than other children. Besides increasing desired behaviors, the Frequent Feedback Procedure shapes adult focus and frequency of interaction to potentially promote change. It may not be sufficient to wait until the end of a period or activity to inform the child about performance; rather, it may be more effective to give feedback more frequently (e.g., every two to three minutes). This feedback can be verbal or in the form of a predetermined nonverbal gesture (e.g., a wink or a thumbs-up sign).

The frequency of feedback should be related directly to the rate of occurrence of the target behavior, as determined by baseline data. For example, if baseline data on a child's interrupting indicate that the child interrupts once every 12 minutes, then feedback should be given more frequently than the problem behavior (e.g., once every 10 minutes). The feedback may target nonoccurrence of the problem behavior or occurrence of a behavior incompatible with the problem behavior.

Before you use the procedure, answer the questions on the Frequent Feedback Form about the behaviors. Each time you use the procedure, place a checkmark in the appropriate box on the form.

Frequent Feedback Form

Child's name _____ Date _____

Form completed by _____

1. What appropriate behavior(s) will be observed? _____

_____

2. What period or activity will the behavior(s) be observed? _____

3. What will be the nature of the feedback? _____

4. Who will be giving the feedback? _____

5. How often will the feedback be given? _____

6. Specific instances in which the behavior(s) will be expected? _____

_____

WEEK 1

Monday	☐	☐	☐	☐	☐	☐	☐	☐	☐	☐
Tuesday	☐	☐	☐	☐	☐	☐	☐	☐	☐	☐
Wednesday	☐	☐	☐	☐	☐	☐	☐	☐	☐	☐
Thursday	☐	☐	☐	☐	☐	☐	☐	☐	☐	☐
Friday	☐	☐	☐	☐	☐	☐	☐	☐	☐	☐
Saturday	☐	☐	☐	☐	☐	☐	☐	☐	☐	☐
Sunday	☐	☐	☐	☐	☐	☐	☐	☐	☐	☐

WEEK 2

Monday	☐	☐	☐	☐	☐	☐	☐	☐	☐	☐
Tuesday	☐	☐	☐	☐	☐	☐	☐	☐	☐	☐
Wednesday	☐	☐	☐	☐	☐	☐	☐	☐	☐	☐
Thursday	☐	☐	☐	☐	☐	☐	☐	☐	☐	☐
Friday	☐	☐	☐	☐	☐	☐	☐	☐	☐	☐
Saturday	☐	☐	☐	☐	☐	☐	☐	☐	☐	☐
Sunday	☐	☐	☐	☐	☐	☐	☐	☐	☐	☐

From *The Behavior Problems Resource Kit,* © 2010 by Michael J. Asher, Steven B. Gordon, Michael C. Selbst, and Mark Cooperberg, Champaign, IL: Research Press (800-519-2707, www.researchpress.com)

Rule Establishment Procedure

Children and adolescents with disruptive behavior problems also at times have trouble with rule-governed behavior. Children with either internalizing or externalizing disorders can benefit from review of expectations. This procedure is designed to help them follow rules in high-risk situations. Two to four rules for each high-risk situation are developed; these rules are then discussed with the child before the situation occurs. Any number of individuals may be involved in following up the procedure: parents, teachers and school support staff, mental health professionals—even the child's peers.

It is important for the rules to be specific, observable, positive, and anchored to a discrete situation (e.g., playground, independent seatwork, arrival home from school, homework). Framing the rules in a positive way is especially important—for instance, Rule 1 in Sample 1 is a positive way of saying, "Do not hit."

You may use the Rule Establishment Form, then write the high-risk situation and related rules on 3 × 5–inch cards. You can make mutliple cards and laminate them if you wish. Several examples follow.

Sample 1

Situation:	_Standing in line_
Rule 1.	_Keep hands and feet by your side._
Rule 2.	_Stand quietly._
Rule 3.	_Wait for the teacher to give the signal to go._

Sample 2

Situation:	_Going to the grocery store_
Rule 1.	_Walk when in the store._
Rule 2.	_Stay close to parent._
Rule 3.	_Keep hands and feet by your side._
Rule 4.	_Ask parent permission before touching a store item._

Sample 3

> ### Recess Rule Card: Robert
>
> *I'm heading out to recess. I need to remember:*
>
> 1. *to speak and act respectfully towards others.*
>
> 2. *to act nicely and keep my hands to myself.*
>
> 3. *to give other students space and be as nice as possible.*
>
> 4. *to share activities and give others opportunities to play.*

Sample 4

> ### Billy's Classroom Rules
>
> 1. *I will sit at my desk and do my work.*
>
> 2. *I will raise my hand before I leave my seat.*
>
> 3. *I will not bother or annoy others.*
>
> 4. *I will keep my hands and feet to myself.*
>
> 5. *I will try to complete the class work I am assigned.*

Sample 5

> ### Activity Monitoring: Angela
>
> ### Activity or task I will complete: _____
>
> *Behaviors I will use to be successful:*
>
> 1. *I will use words to express my feelings.*
>
> 2. *I will listen and follow my teacher's directions.*
>
> 3. *If I have a problem, I will ask for help.*

Rule Establishment Form

Child's name _____ Week of _____

Form completed by _____

High-risk situation _____

Rules identified to be followed:

Rule 1. _____

Rule 2. _____

Rule 3. _____

Rule 4. _____

Rule 5. _____

From *The Behavior Problems Resource Kit,* © 2010 by Michael J. Asher, Steven B. Gordon, Michael C. Selbst, and Mark Cooperberg, Champaign, IL: Research Press (800-519-2707, www.researchpress.com)

Rule Review Procedure

Reviewing rules before high-risk situations helps the child or adolescent remember to use them. The Rule Review Procedure involves having the child commit certain rules to memory, then asking the child to name and describe these rules before beginning the activity associated with the rules. The child may memorize several rules pertaining to a single situation, as in the Rule Establishment Procedure, or just one rule—for example, "Use an inside voice when riding in the car."

Review the rules with the child verbally; to keep track of how often you use the procedure, place a checkmark in the appropriate box on the Rule Review Monitoring Form.

Child's name _____ Week of _____

Form completed by _____

	High-risk Situation 1						**High-risk Situation 2**				
	(fill in)						(fill in)				
Monday	☐	☐	☐	☐	☐		☐	☐	☐	☐	☐
Tuesday	☐	☐	☐	☐	☐		☐	☐	☐	☐	☐
Wednesday	☐	☐	☐	☐	☐		☐	☐	☐	☐	☐
Thursday	☐	☐	☐	☐	☐		☐	☐	☐	☐	☐
Friday	☐	☐	☐	☐	☐		☐	☐	☐	☐	☐
Saturday	☐	☐	☐	☐	☐		☐	☐	☐	☐	☐
Sunday	☐	☐	☐	☐	☐		☐	☐	☐	☐	☐

Rule Evaluation Procedure

Evaluating rules after high-risk situations helps children or adolescents examine how well they were able to use them. Self-evaluation of behavior after activities can help children remember and choose to improve their behavior in high-risk situations. Along with self-monitoring and self-reinforcement, self-evaluation is an essential component of self-regulation.

The Rule Evaluation Procedure involves asking the child to provide a rating on how well he or she complied with the rules after the activity associated with the rules ends. The child may be evaluating several rules pertaining to a single event, as in the Rule Establishment Procedure, or just one rule—for example, "Keep your hands and feet to yourself."

With adult assistance, the child can complete a Rule Evaluation Form. Following an activity, the child rates how he or she did in following rules on the standard criteria. The rating scale can be added to rule cards created in the Rule Establishment Procedure. The child can rate performance of the behavior alone, or an adult observer and the child can make separate ratings, as shown in the following examples.

**Sample 1:
Student**

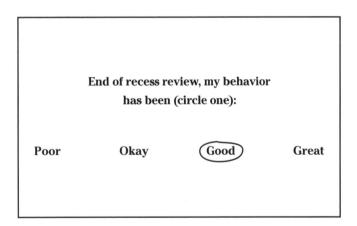

**Sample 2:
Student
and Teacher**

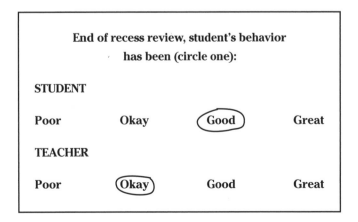

Rule Evaluation Form

Child's name _____ Week of _____

Form completed by _____

High-risk situation _____

Rules identified to be followed:

Rule 1. _____

Rule 2. _____

Rule 3. _____

Rule 4. _____

Rule 5. _____

Criteria for ratings ("How well did you comply with the rules?")

       1 = Poor: Unable to follow rules for most of class period

       2 = Okay: Followed rules for most of period but had major violation

       3 = Good: Followed rules for most of period but had minor violation

       4 = Great: Had few or no difficulties

From *The Behavior Problems Resource Kit,* © 2010 by Michael J. Asher, Steven B. Gordon, Michael C. Selbst, and Mark Cooperberg, Champaign, IL: Research Press (800-519-2707, www.researchpress.com)

Rule Compliance Procedure

The Rule Compliance Procedure establishes the use of positive consequences for adhering to rules. These positive consequences can be in the form of self-reinforcement (e.g., "I did a great job"), social reinforcement (e.g., "You really spoke nicely to the other children during the kickball game"), activity reinforcement (e.g., ten minutes of free time on the computer), symbolic reinforcement (e.g., tokens or points) or tangible reinforcement (e.g., food).

Before using this procedure, it is important to identify meaningful reinforcers for the individual by completing the Reinforcement Inventory for Children or the Reinforcement Inventory for Adolescents (see Appendix A). The Rule Compliance Form guides the child in developing a plan for success and establishing reinforcement. To keep track of your use of the procedure, place a checkmark in the appropriate box on the form.

Rule Compliance Form

Child's name _____ Date _____

Form completed by _____

1. My plan for success is: _____

_____

2. My self-statement for doing a good job is: _____

_____

3. The activity I have chosen for the following the rules is: _____

_____

4. The reward I have chosen for following the rules is: _____

_____

	Week 1						**Week 2**				
Monday	☐	☐	☐	☐	☐		☐	☐	☐	☐	☐
Tuesday	☐	☐	☐	☐	☐		☐	☐	☐	☐	☐
Wednesday	☐	☐	☐	☐	☐		☐	☐	☐	☐	☐
Thursday	☐	☐	☐	☐	☐		☐	☐	☐	☐	☐
Friday	☐	☐	☐	☐	☐		☐	☐	☐	☐	☐
Saturday	☐	☐	☐	☐	☐		☐	☐	☐	☐	☐
Sunday	☐	☐	☐	☐	☐		☐	☐	☐	☐	☐

From *The Behavior Problems Resource Kit,* © 2010 by Michael J. Asher, Steven B. Gordon, Michael C. Selbst, and Mark Cooperberg, Champaign, IL: Research Press (800-519-2707, www.researchpress.com)

Rule Violation Procedures

Rule Violation Procedures vary according to the age of the child and whether the setting is school or home. To keep track of your use of the procedure, use the Rule Violation Monitoring Form–School or the Rule Violation Monitoring Form–Home, as appropriate.

RULE VIOLATION—PRIMARY GRADES

This Rule Violation Procedure is intended for school use and establishes in advance that the child will receive a yellow card (as a reminder to the child to be cautious) the first time a rule violation occurs. The second time a rule violation occurs, the child receives a red card, meaning the child is removed from the area and placed in "Sit and Watch." The Sit and Watch procedure involves the following steps.

Sit and Watch

Step 1: The child sits away from the activity while the adult states the rule that was violated and asks the child to repeat it. The adult informs the child of the need to sit and watch how the other children follow the rule.

Step 2: While the child watches, the adult makes a point of praising other children for rule compliance.

Step 3: At the end of three to five minutes, after the child has remained calm, the adult asks the child to state the rule and say what he or she should have done instead. The child then returns to the activity.

Step 4: When the child returns to the activity, the adult offers praise for rule compliance.

Note: Some children may need coaching or a brief role play in order to respond correctly to the Sit and Watch procedure.

RULE VIOLATION—SECONDARY GRADES

This Rule Violation Procedure intended for school use establishes in advance that the child will receive a yellow card (a reminder to be cautious) the first time a rule violation occurs. The second time a rule violation occurs, the child receives a red card, meaning the child is removed from the area. The child is isolated for 5 to 10 minutes, and then given an opportunity to return after completing a Stop and Think Planning Essay (see p. 172) as well as any missed schoolwork.

Before using the procedure with either age group, ask yourself the following questions. If you answer "no" to any questions, address these issues.

1. Has a warning signal been established?

2. Has the method been adequately explained to the student?

3. Has the method been adequately explained to the class?

4. Has parent cooperation been obtained?

5. Has administrative support been obtained?

Each time you use the procedure, place a check mark in the appropriate box on the Rule Violation Monitoring Form–School.

RULE VIOLATION—HOME (CHILDREN TO AGE 12)

This home procedure establishes in advance that the child will receive a yellow card (a reminder to be cautious) the first time a rule violation occurs. The second time a rule violation occurs, the child receives a red card, meaning the child is removed from the area and is placed in "Sit and Think." The Sit and Think procedure involves the following steps.

Sit and Think

Step 1: The child is directed to sit in a semi-secluded area (e.g., the bottom step of the front hall) while the adult states the rule that was violated. The adult informs the child of the need to sit and think about how to follow the rule.

Step 2: Sit and Think begins when the child is sitting properly and quietly. At the end of three to five minutes, after the child has remained calm, the adult approaches and asks the child to state the rule that was violated and what he or she should do instead.

Step 3: When the child returns to general household activities, the adult offers praise for rule compliance.

Note: Some children may need coaching or a brief role play in order to respond correctly to the Sit and Think procedure.

RULE VIOLATION—HOME (CHILDREN OVER AGE 12)

This home procedure establishes in advance that the child will receive a yellow card (a reminder to be cautious) the first time a rule violation occurs. The second time a rule violation occurs, the child receives a red card and a response cost procedure is imposed—in other words, the child loses a significant item (e.g., computer, telephone, etc.) upon the occurrence of a rule violation. After 24 hours, the child is given an opportunity to have the item returned after having completed a Stop and Think Planning Essay (see p. 172).

Ask yourself the following questions. If you answer any "no" to any questions, address these issues before using the procedure.

1. Has a warning signal been established?

2. Has the method been adequately explained to the child?

3. Has the method been adequately explained to other family members?

4. Have both parents agreed to implement this strategy?

Each time you use the procedure, place a checkmark in the appropriate box on the Rule Violation Monitoring Form–Home.

Rule Violation Monitoring Form–School

Student's name _____ Date _____

Form completed by _____

Rule 1

_____
(fill in)

Monday	☐	☐	☐	☐	☐
Tuesday	☐	☐	☐	☐	☐
Wednesday	☐	☐	☐	☐	☐
Thursday	☐	☐	☐	☐	☐
Friday	☐	☐	☐	☐	☐

Rule 2

_____
(fill in)

Monday	☐	☐	☐	☐	☐
Tuesday	☐	☐	☐	☐	☐
Wednesday	☐	☐	☐	☐	☐
Thursday	☐	☐	☐	☐	☐
Friday	☐	☐	☐	☐	☐

From *The Behavior Problems Resource Kit,* © 2010 by Michael J. Asher, Steven B. Gordon, Michael C. Selbst, and Mark Cooperberg, Champaign, IL: Research Press (800-519-2707, www.researchpress.com)

Rule Violation Monitoring Form–Home

Child's name _____ Date _____

Form completed by _____

	Rule 1 _____ (fill in)	**Rule 2** _____ (fill in)
Monday	☐ ☐ ☐ ☐ ☐	☐ ☐ ☐ ☐ ☐
Tuesday	☐ ☐ ☐ ☐ ☐	☐ ☐ ☐ ☐ ☐
Wednesday	☐ ☐ ☐ ☐ ☐	☐ ☐ ☐ ☐ ☐
Thursday	☐ ☐ ☐ ☐ ☐	☐ ☐ ☐ ☐ ☐
Friday	☐ ☐ ☐ ☐ ☐	☐ ☐ ☐ ☐ ☐
Saturday	☐ ☐ ☐ ☐ ☐	☐ ☐ ☐ ☐ ☐
Sunday	☐ ☐ ☐ ☐ ☐	☐ ☐ ☐ ☐ ☐

Educational Accommodation Plan Form

Child's name _____ Date _____

Age _____ Grade _____

Form completed by _____

School _____

Form completed by _____

Reason for eligibility _____

Identified difficulties _____

_____

Effect on student's education _____

_____

Place a checkmark next to the accommodations that would be helpful for the student. This list is meant as a guide for accommodations in the general education classroom and is not intended to be exhaustive. Please list other accommodations as appropriate.

Physical aspects of the classroom

☐ Stand near the student when lessons are being given.

☐ Identify student's education difficulties.

☐ Be aware the student may need frequent help with _____.

☐ Allow the student to sit next to another student who can provide assistance.

☐ Allow the student to sit near the front of the room and/or near good role models.

☐ Seat the student away from distractions.

☐ Vary classroom arrangements, allowing the student to move between learning stations.

☐ Allow teacher to place desks in rows rather than clusters and increase distance between desks.

☐ Make specific arrangements if the student has trouble copying from the board.

From *The Behavior Problems Resource Kit,* © 2010 by Michael J. Asher, Steven B. Gordon, Michael C. Selbst, and Mark Cooperberg, Champaign, IL: Research Press (800-519-2707, www.researchpress.com)

☐ Post a schedule of daily lessons and activities and announce changes in routines.

☐ Post the rules or classroom expectations.

☐ Post homework assignments in the same place every day.

☐ Provide assistance in note taking.

☐ Increase adult support and supervision.

☐ Allow student to be member of in-school support class or use a classroom aide to increase supervision.

☐ Provide student with amplification system to increase volume of staff's voice when deemed helpful.

☐ Allow student to use cell phone to photograph information on board.

☐ Other _____

☐ Other _____

How will these accommodations be operationalized? Be specific in your descriptions so that others may understand how to implement these modifications.

_____

_____

_____

Lesson presentation

☐ Consider the skills needed to engage the lesson presented.

☐ Vary the content of lessons in amount, duration, and conceptual level.

☐ Vary the style of presentation, including audiovisual, demonstration, written, tactile, and verbal modes.

☐ Increase visual aids to provide lesson content and examples.

☐ Tell the student the purpose of the lesson as well as the expectations during the lesson.

☐ Obtain frequent student responses and input.

☐ Make lessons brief; break longer lessons into short segments.

☐ Divide tasks into parts; give one part at a time.

☐ Allow for someone to check the student's class work frequently.

☐ Provide organizational aids for student to follow when possible.

☐ Allow frequent breaks; vary activities often.

☐ Involve the student in demonstrating lesson content.

☐ Permit audiotaping of lectures and discussions.

☐ Allow the use of adaptive equipment such as calculators and spell-checkers.

☐ Provide a note taker or a copy of another student's (or the instructor's) notes.

☐ Cue the student before asking questions, allow for think time, and then call on the student.

☐ Help the student learn to ask for help.

☐ Provide more individualized instruction or assistance compared to typical students.

☐ Repeat and rephrasing questions or directions.

☐ Have student review key points orally when possible.

☐ Provide student with outline of lecture during class.

☐ Include reading or talking aloud to improve comprehension.

☐ Increase use of differentiated instruction to address students' individual style.

☐ Increase use of computer-assisted instruction.

☐ Other _____

☐ Other _____

How will these accommodations be operationalized? Be specific in your descriptions so that others may understand how to implement these modifications.

_____

_____

_____

Assignments

☐ Provide only short, clear instructions.

☐ Provide oral along with written directions for the student's later reference.

☐ Check in often with the student; have him or her repeat directions.

☐ Break down and simplify complex instructions.

☐ Adjust time for completion of assignments; allow extensions if necessary.

☐ Monitor the student for follow through on lengthy assignments; help the student establish timelines.

☐ Provide graphic organizer for writing assignments.

☐ Hand out assignments or worksheets one at a time.

☐ Accept work whether it is complete or not.

☐ Reduce quantity and focus on quality.

☐ Reduce complexity of reading level of assigned tasks.

☐ Do not grade homework assignments down for spelling and sentence structure errors (unless that is the purpose of the assignment).

☐ Modify homework expectations and slowly increase expectations across the school year.

☐ Use an individualized grading system.

☐ Allow the student to use means other than writing to exhibit work (e.g., oral presentations).

☐ Set up a time for morning check-in for rapport building and organization of desk and bag.

☐ Set up a time for afternoon check-out regarding student's needs, mood, and/or behavior.

☐ Develop an assignment sheet to be kept by the student and checked by a teacher or peer tutor.

☐ Develop an organizational checklist for work and books.

☐ Present required reading on audiotape.

☐ Provide assistance in highlighting main concepts in written material.

☐ Supply the student with examples of expected work.

☐ Accept work typed, dictated, or tape recorded (by others if needed).

☐ Provide a resource for the student to obtain help to organize other responsibilities (e.g., assign the student to last period study hall).

☐ Provide the student with an after-school tutor to help complete assigned homework.

☐ Provide more individualized instruction or assistance compared to typical student.

☐ Provide the student with a second set of textbooks for home use.

☐ Allow parents to limit homework assignments if evening homework duration becomes excessive.

☐ Help the student's parents structure study time at home.

☐ Apprise the student's parents about any long-term assignments.

☐ Provide homework planner to be reviewed and signed by staff and parent.

☐ Provide visual prompts to help student write neatly (e.g., spacing, staying on lines).

☐ Include the use of hands-on materials (manipulatives).

☐ Help to color-code folders to better organize materials.

☐ Provide peer support to assist with organizational needs.

☐ Assign and reward volunteer study buddy.

☐ Develop a checklist for completion of assignments (e.g., topic sentence, spelling/punctuation).

☐ Allow student to use electronic or graphic organizer for writing assignments.

☐ Include the use of assistive technology for class assignments (e.g., keyboard, audiotape).

□ When possible, close open tasks (e.g., provide sentence starters, fill in the blank, multiple choice).

□ Allow student to include specific areas of interest when doing assignments when possible.

□ Include the use of Cue and Review Procedure (p. 152) as a means of cognitive rehearsal.

□ Devise and use a self-monitoring system.

□ Provide student with one-to-one support to plan, organize, and follow through with task demands.

□ Other _____

□ Other _____

How will these accommodations be operationalized? Be specific in your descriptions so that others may understand how to implement these modifications.

_____

_____

_____

Test taking

□ Provide increased time for tests.

□ Allow the student to retake tests when performance is poor.

□ Give student more frequent short quizzes to replace longer tests.

□ Allow alternative means for exhibiting mastery (e.g., take-home tests).

□ Vary the means of class evaluation to ensure that the student has an opportunity to succeed.

□ Give tests and quizzes orally.

□ Permit student to provide test answers on a tape recorder.

□ Modify testing format.

□ Allow the student to take tests in alternative settings to meet specific needs.

□ Read test items to student when reading is not the area being assessed.

□ Modify district-state testing requirements.

□ Provide the student with a sample or practice test when possible.

□ Provide all possible test questions and have the student and teacher select specific items and number.

□ Allow student to contribute test questions in advance.

□ Allow open-book or open-notes tests.

☐ Other _____

☐ Other _____

How will these accommodations be operationalized? Be specific in your descriptions so that others may understand how to implement these modifications.

_____

_____

_____

Behavior/discipline

☐ Plan for problems; be aware of possible frustrating situations.

☐ Allow for a cooling-off period.

☐ Ignore inappropriate behavior as much as possible.

☐ Train in a "keep calm" procedure.

☐ Modify school disciplinary code to address student's behavioral issues.

☐ Ensure that a target behavior is reinforced to replace the problem behaviors being punished.

☐ Expand the disciplinary procedure to include fines, restitution, and community service.

☐ Provide the student with an ongoing coaching program to assist throughout the school day.

☐ Use a behavior management program such as the School Environment Learning Program (SELP) to monitor and reinforce behavior throughout the school day. (See pp. 176).

☐ Provide the student with more frequent behavior-specific praise compared to typical student.

☐ Increase frequency and immediacy or reward system to promote work completion.

☐ Make necessary staff available to monitor on field trips.

☐ Provide staff with inservice training on student's disability.

☐ Develop and implement a positive behavior intervention plan.

☐ Increase support and supervision of student in unstructured setting and on bus.

☐ Provide student with school-based counseling.

☐ Accommodate specific dietary needs.

☐ Other _____

☐ Other _____

How will these accommodations be operationalized? Be specific in your descriptions so that others may understand how to implement these modifications.

_____

_____

_____

Other (e.g., medication, counseling, social skills training)

☐ Monitor administration of medication.

☐ Report medication effects to physician and parents.

☐ Complete frequent rating scales for medication monitoring.

☐ Set time aside to build a rapport with the student; schedule regular times to check in and talk.

☐ Avoid embarrassing situations that require the student to read aloud or respond to questions when unprepared.

☐ Develop and help the student stick to a daily routine.

☐ Frequently reinforce the student's strengths and successes.

☐ Develop a buddy system to assist in getting around school, completing homework assignments, taking notes, and participating in recreational activities such as recess.

☐ Provide the student with a social skills group.

☐ Modify length of school day.

☐ Other _____

☐ Other _____

How will these accommodations be operationalized? Be specific in your descriptions so that others may understand how to implement these modifications.

_____

_____

_____

Persons responsible for implementing and monitoring the accommodations

School district's representative _____

Guidance counselor_____

Counselor/social worker _____

Classroom teacher_____

Other _____

Ongoing communication between home, school, and outside agencies

☐ Modify parent communication (increase frequency).

☐ Schedule periodic parent-teacher meetings.

☐ Send home daily/weekly progress reports.

☐ Develop plans to include the input of physicians, psychologists, or other mental health professionals.

How will these accommodations be operationalized? Be specific in your descriptions so that others may understand how to implement these modifications.

_____

_____

_____

BEHAVIORAL INTERVENTIONS: TEACHING REPLACEMENT BEHAVIORS

Feelings Management

Feelings management provides the child with the skills to manage emotions effectively. The accompanying forms provide an overview of strategies that help children calm down when they are upset. A variety of strategies have been developed and utilitzed by the authors of this book, and these were creatively organized to form an acronym (STOP AND COPE). These strategies are effective with anger, frustration, sadness, or anxiety. The model includes many strategies here because the more options that exist, the greater the likelihood of a favorable outcome. These coping strategies have been taught to hundreds of people in schools and in the therapy room, both in individual and group settings.

The Feelings Management Handout can be used as an intervention tool by following the 3-D Skills Approach (see p. 134): First the clinician *discusses* the importance of managing feelings. Children are instructed that "Everyone gets upset sometimes. What matters is how you act when you are upset." Thus a distinction between feelings and behaviors is made. The goal is not to eliminate upsetting emotions, but to promote effective coping. Next the clinician *demonstrates* how to use each strategy. For example, when teaching a child to walk away from a dangerous interpersonal confrontation, the clinician should actually demonstrate walking away from a feelings trigger. Finally, the child is provided the opportunity to *do* the skill by acting out the effective strategy. In many cases, the child will need guidance from the clinician to perform the behavior in an appropriate fashion. The clinician should use generous positive feedback and praise. For example, "I really like the way that you are breathing through your nose. Please make sure to breath out through your mouth . . . That's it, way to go!"

In many cases, it is not possible to eliminate the feelings entirely, so it is recommended that the child first be asked to identify and then rate the feeling on a numerical scale. For example, a child may state, "I feel angry an 8 out of 10." Rating upsetting feelings shows the child that there are different intensities of emotions, which is important because effective coping strategies are more likely to reduce the intensity of a specified feeling (e.g., angry 8 out of 10 reduced to 3 out of 10) than to change the feeling to a different emotional state (e.g., angry to happy).

After the Feelings Management Handout is the Feelings Management Project, which describes a four-step process to help the child cope with feelings. The first page lists the steps and gives an example. The second page provides two forms that the child can fill out after experiencing a triggering event. The clinician can assist the child in filling in at least one of the two forms before asking the child to fill out the form independently. In addition to having the child fill out the Feelings Management Project after experiencing an upsetting event, clinicians may elect to utilize prevention methods to identify high-risk situations for a child and create a plan identifying which strategies that child may use when upset. For example, a child may find playing basketball in gym class to be a high-risk situation, because he has difficulty managing his anger when he loses. The clinician can help map out a plan to (a) stop what you are doing and take a break, (b) take deep breaths, and (c) refocus to think about the next game.

The final form in this section is the Learning My Feelings Log. With the help of an adult, the child walks through the course of an event beginning with the trigger to their emotional reactions. Then the child addresses the *what, who, where* and *when* of the situation. The child identifies the feeling and rates its level of intensity, then describes what behavior he or she chose in response to that feeling. With repeated practice, the child will be better able to associate the level of distress for a given problem situation with outcomes and plan to use better coping strategies next time.

Feelings Management helps people learn to recognize, understand, and manage their feelings. Everyone gets upset sometimes. What matters is how you act when you are upset. Remember when you are upset, STOP AND COPE.

S—Stop what you're doing and take a break.

- Remove yourself from your feelings trigger.

- Separate yourself from the person or situation that has led you to feel upset.

- Sometimes getting a drink helps to cool your feelings.

T—Take deep breaths.

- Take 3 slow, deep breaths.

- Breathe in through nose for 5 seconds.

- Hold it for 2 seconds.

- Breathe out through mouth for 5 seconds.

O—Okay to walk away.

- Tell yourself it is okay to let it go and walk away from the feelings trigger.

P—Pick something fun to do.

- If you are doing something you like, it is hard to be upset.

- Watch a funny movie or TV show, play a fun game or sport.

A—Analyze your thoughts.

- Identify and challenge your negative thoughts. Are you telling yourself the truth?

- How big a deal is this? Will it matter in a week? A year? Is this a helpful thought?

N—New focus.

- Change your focus to something more positive—something you are looking forward to doing or something you experienced in the past that you enjoyed.

- Change your thoughts away from the trigger and onto something else. Read a book, magazine, or article, or think about a preferred hobby or interest.

D—Draw or write.

- Draw or write to express yourself.

From *The Behavior Problems Resource Kit,* © 2010 by Michael J. Asher, Steven B. Gordon, Michael C. Selbst, and Mark Cooperberg, Champaign, IL: Research Press (800-519-2707, www.researchpress.com)

C—Count backwards slowly.

- 10, 9, 8, 7, 6, 5, 4, 3, 2, 1. Your focus will shift to the numbers, rather than the feelings trigger.

O—Open up to a friend or relative.

- Get help by sharing your feelings with someone.

P—Problem solve.

- Once you are calm, you can solve your problem by following the problem-solving steps: name the problem, brainstorm solutions, evaluate solutions, choose a solution, make a plan, do it.

E—Exercise!

Release your physical energy/stress by walking, jogging, or other exercise.

Feelings Management Handout (page 2 of 2)

This project will help you to learn to cope with your feelings. If you use one of the strategies from the Feelings Management Handout, you will be likely to feel better. Please get help if you need it.

STEPS

1. Identify your **feelings trigger.**

2. Identify your feeling or **emotional consequence** and rate it on a scale of 1 to 10.

3. Identify the **coping strategies** you can use.

4. Check to see if your coping strategies **worked**—identify and rate your feeling again.

Here's an example . . .

1. My **feelings trigger** (What happened?)

   I have a big test in math tomorrow!

2. My **emotional consequence** (I feel *really nervous.)*

   Rating: A *9* out of 10.

3. My **coping strategies**

   I can <u>take deep breaths</u> and try to relax. I will also <u>open up to</u> my dad and get his help. He is good at math.

4. Did my coping strategies **work?**

   I now feel better, but still a little nervous.

   Rating: A *3* out of 10.

Remember the STOP AND COPE strategies . . .

S—Stop what you are doing and take a break.

T—Take deep breaths.

O—Okay to walk away.

P—Pick something fun to do.

A—Analyze your thoughts.

N—New focus.

D—Draw or write.

C—Count backwards slowly. 10, 9, 8, 7, 6, 5, 4, 3, 2, 1

O—Open up to a friend or relative.

P—Problem solve.

E—Exercise!

Event 1

1. My **feelings trigger** (What happened?)

   _____

   _____

2. My **emotional consequence** (I feel _____)

   Rating: A _____ out of 10.

3. My **coping strategies**

   _____

   _____

4. Did my coping strategies **work?** (I now feel _____)

   Rating: A _____ out of 10.

   _____

Event 2

1. My **feelings trigger** (What happened?)

   _____

   _____

2. My **emotional consequence** (I feel _____)

   Rating: A _____ out of 10.

3. My **coping strategies** (remember STOP AND COPE)

   _____

   _____

4. Did my coping strategies **work?** (I now feel _____)

   Rating: A _____ out of 10.

Learning My Feelings Log

Child's name _____ Date _____

Form completed by _____

What happened?

☐ Somebody teased me.
☐ Somebody took something of mine.
☐ Somebody told me to do something.
☐ Somebody was doing something I didn't like.
☐ Somebody started fighting with me.
☐ Other _____

Who was that somebody?

☐ Another child
☐ Teacher
☐ Parent
☐ Another adult
☐ Sister/brother
☐ Other _____

Where were you?

☐ Classroom   ☐ Lunchroom   ☐ Playground   ☐ Street
☐ Hallway   ☐ Bathroom   ☐ House   ☐ Other _____

How did you feel?

☐ Happy   ☐ Sad   ☐ Scared   ☐ Embarrassed   ☐ Mad

How strong were your feelings? (circle best choice)

1 2 3 4 5 6 7 8 9 10
Weak   Medium   Strong

What did you do? (check all that apply)

☐ Hit, pushed, kicked
☐ Screamed
☐ Ran away
☐ Cried
☐ Threw something
☐ Broke something

☐ Told adult
☐ Walked away
☐ Talked it out calmly
☐ Told another child
☐ Ignored
☐ Other _____

How did you handle yourself?   ☐ Poorly   ☐ Not so well   ☐ Okay   ☐ Good   ☐ Great

What will you do next time?

My plan is to _____

From *The Behavior Problems Resource Kit,* © 2010 by Michael J. Asher, Steven B. Gordon, Michael C. Selbst, and Mark Cooperberg, Champaign, IL: Research Press (800-519-2707, www.researchpress.com)

Happening-Thoughts-Feeling-Reactions

Happening-Thoughts-Feeling-Reactions (HFTR) is based on the thinking-feeling connection. The child is provided with the skills to understand the connection between thoughts and feelings and to become more effective at managing emotions. This model was adapted from Dr. Albert Ellis's Rational Emotive Behavior Therapy (REBT). REBT is a type of cognitive-behavior therapy to assist individuals with their moods and anxiety. The individual learns to make the connection between thoughts and resulting emotional reactions. Simply put, our thoughts lead directly to our feelings: Thoughts → emotions and behaviors. Irrational thoughts can lead to negative emotional states, such as depression and anxiety. While this intervention is complex, it has the benefit of producing possible life-long changes in children who may be capable of modulating their affect by changing their thoughts.

First, help the child understand that thoughts lead to feelings. Here is a common example: Two students are walking in a crowded school hallway. They bump into one another. The first child says to himself, "The hallway is really crowded. I need to watch where I'm going." The second child says to himself, "That guy is a jerk. He needs to watch where he is going, or he is going to regret it!" These two students experience the same event, but they have different thoughts about it. As a result of his thought, the first student is not very bothered by bumping into the second student. The second student, however, is very angry because he believes that it occurred as the result of a hostile action. These thoughts result in different feelings in each of the students.

Once the connection between thoughts and feelings has been made, children learn to identify thoughts by talking (or writing down) their beliefs. After the children identify thoughts, they learn to react to troublesome thoughts by challenging the thought with several questions. A series of questions guide the child (and relevant caregivers) to challenge thoughts and create a more helpful replacement thought. These are the questions:

1. Where is the evidence that my thought is true?

2. How big a deal is this?

3. Is this a helpful thought? If not, what could I think instead?

In the first question, the children learn to check to see if they have "evidence" to support their conclusions. One developmental adaptation of this question includes instruction in truth telling. The child is asked, "What do you call someone who tells you things that aren't true?" Most young children quickly respond, "A liar." The child is then asked, "What would you be if you told yourself something that wasn't true?" The child responds, "A liar." Then the child is asked, "Do you want to be a liar?" Of course, children respond that they do not want to be a liar. The clinician then instructs the child to make sure that you are not a liar and that you are telling the truth to yourself. Children are instructed to look for proof that they are telling the truth. This may be expressed to the children as being a "detective" who is looking for evidence of the truth. If children don't have evidence to support their belief, they have committed a "thought crime" and need to correct the belief.

In some instances, children may have evidence that their thought is true (e.g., Yes, someone did push you). The child is then directed to ask the second question, "How big a deal is this?" This question helps the child to put things into perspective. It is often helpful to have the child rate how big a deal something is on a scale of 1 to 10. Most children benefit from a discussion of various anchor points (or reference points), such as "Getting the blue instead of the red marker is not a big deal . . . it is a 2 out of 10 . . . but getting run over by a bus would be a 10 out of 10." Humor or exaggeration often helps the child to understand the concepts and to engage in the intervention. For example, the clinician may question a child who says that losing his baseball game is a 10 out of 10 by falling on the floor and gasping for air, stating, "My team lost the game . . . I can't breathe . . . I'm going to die." Children can see that they are making too big a deal out of the game that they lost. Learning how to rate how big a deal something is sets a limit on how strong the resulting feeling might be. If something is deemed to be a 5 out of 10 on the big deal scale, the emotional reaction might be limited to a 5 out of 10. While this intervention may provide the child with a different feeling, in many cases it is more likely the child will simply feel less of a certain feeling (going from an angry 8 to an angry 3).

The next question may be necessary when children do have evidence that their thought is true, and it is also a big deal. For example, a child could say, "There are children starving in third world countries." This belief has truth, and most people would consider this a big deal. Obviously, being aware of this and helping by making a donation might be helpful, but spending time worrying about this is not productive. Through this intervention, children may learn that their thoughts, while true, may not be helpful to themselves.

Children as young as seven years old can complete this process. However, children in early elementary school may initially struggle to grasp the concepts. Repetition and review of the concepts, along with use of the 3-D Skills Approach (p. 134), can be helpful.

This strategy is particularly effective with children in middle and high school who struggle with anger, frustration, sadness, or anxiety. While no child is expected to have success during every trial, children who practice the strategy can ultimately succeed.

The Happening-Thoughts-Feeling-Reactions Project provides an overview of the process. The first page of the handout lists the steps and gives an example. The second page provides two forms that the child can fill out after experiencing a triggering event. The clinician may assist the child in filling in at least one of the two forms before asking the child to fill out a form independently. It is recommended that until a child shows mastery of identifying thoughts first, he or she be instructed to identify feelings first, then thoughts.

This project will help you learn to argue with thoughts that cause you problems and replace them with more helpful ones. If you follow these steps, you will likely feel better. Please get help if you need it.

STEPS

1. Identify the **happening.** (Answer the question "What happened?")

2. Identify your **thought** or belief. (Answer the question "What am I thinking, or what was I thinking?")

3. Identify your **feeling** and rate it on a scale of 1 to 10.

4. Check your **reaction.** (Be a good detective and answer the following questions.)

   Where is the evidence that my thought is true?

   How big a deal is this? (Rate it on a 1 to 10 scale.)

   Is this a helpful thought? If not, what could I think to myself instead?

After you answer these questions, identify your feeling again and rate it from 1 to 10.

Here's an example . . .

1. My **happening**

   Jenna ran into me in the hallway.

2. My **thought** or belief

   Jenna ran into me on purpose. She is such a big jerk!

3. My **feeling**

   I feel blazing hot angry. Rating: A 9 out of 10.

4. My **reaction**

   Is there evidence that my thought is true? *No.*

   How big a deal is this? Rating: *A 2 out of 10. After all, Jenna didn't break my arm or anything!*

   Is this a helpful thought? If not, what could I think instead?

   I don't know that Jenna ran into me on purpose. The hallway gets crowded between classes.

   I now feel *a little annoyed. Rating: A 2 out of 10.*

From *The Behavior Problems Resource Kit,* © 2010 by Michael J. Asher, Steven B. Gordon, Michael C. Selbst, and Mark Cooperberg, Champaign, IL: Research Press (800-519-2707, www.researchpress.com)

Event 1

1. My **happening**

_____

2. My **thought** or belief

_____

3. My **feeling** (I feel _____)

    Rating: A _____ out of 10.

4. My **reaction**

    Is there evidence that my thought is true?

    How big a deal is this? Rating: A _____ out of 10.

    Is this a helpful thought? If not, what could I think instead?

    _____

I now feel _____ Rating: A _____ out of 10.

Event 2

1. My **happening**

_____

2. My **thought** or belief

_____

3. My **feeling** (I feel _____)

    Rating: A _____ out of 10.

4. My **reaction**

    Is there evidence that my thought is true?

    How big a deal is this? Rating: A _____ out of 10.

    Is this a helpful thought? If not, what could I think instead?

    _____

I now feel _____ Rating: A _____ out of 10.

How to Solve a Problem (HOTSAP)

How to Solve a Problem, or HOTSAP, is a ten-step problem-solving approach. HOTSAP works best when the child is calm and not in a moment of crisis. The approach requires a positive working relationship between the adult and the child. The catchy acronym HOTSAP is readily incorporated into discussions with children—for example, "Let's use HOTSAP" or "Do you think HOTSAP might help?"

HOTSAP focuses on facets within the individual (e.g., cognitive and behavioral repertoires and predisposition to respond to potentially problematic situations), as well as external and interactional events (e.g., antecedents and consequences from others) to promote prosocial behavior. The emphasis of HOTSAP is on changing performance at home, at school, and in the community. The clinician teaches HOTSAP for use outside the sessions. The child, parent, and teacher practice separate but interrelated activities and strategies learned in the treatment sessions.

First, the emphasis is on how children approach situations (i.e., the thought processes that guide responses to interpersonal situations). Children are taught to engage in a step-by-step approach to solve interpersonal problems. They make statements to themselves that direct attention to certain aspects of the problem or tasks, the emotional impact, and evaluative skills that eventually lead to effective solutions. Then, target behaviors are selected that are specific to the child's life. As the child's skills improve, the cognitive problem solving skills are increasingly applied to real-life situations.

Therapist, teachers, and parents play an active role in this treatment approach. As part of the problem-solving process, the adult continues to model the cognitive processes by making verbal self-statements, applying the sequence of statements to particular problems, providing cues to prompt use of the skills, and delivering feedback and praise to develop correct use of the skills. Eventually, treatment combines several procedures, including modeling and practice, role playing, and positive and negative consequences to develop increasingly complex response repertoires of the child. An emphasis is placed on delivery of behavior-specific praise and corrective feedback, child self-monitoring and self-appraisal, and review of the child's performance.

For each item on the HOTSAP Form, the adult prompts the child verbally and nonverbally to guide performance, provides a rich schedule of contingent social reinforcement, delivers concrete feedback for performance, and models improved ways of performing. If the child is sufficiently mature, form completion may be self-directed.

Sample HOTSAP Form

Child's name ___Robert_____ Date ___September 24_____

Form completed by _____Mr. Paradise and Robert_____

1. What is your problem?

   ___I want to be successful in school, but I have trouble sitting still, paying attention, following___

   ___directions, and getting organized.___

2. What is your goal or desired end result?

   ___To be successful in school without having too much trouble.___

3. What are your current feelings (angry, scared, sad, embarrassed, etc.)? _____

   ___Frustrated, disappointed, bored.___

4. How strong are your feelings on a 1 (very weak) to 10 (very strong) scale? ___8_____

5. List as many solutions as you can think of that have a good chance of solving the problem and helping you reach your stated goal.

   + ___Ask my teacher for help.___

   + ___Work with my counselor or therapist to learn to pay attention better.___

   + ___Put my papers in my folders.___

   − ___Put my head down and quit working.___

   + ___Keep my eyes focused on my teacher and the board.___

6. Review each solution and decide if it is a good idea, bad idea, and why. Put a plus sign (+) next to the solution if it is a good idea. Put a minus sign (–) next to the solution if it is a bad idea.

7. Circle the solution or solutions you feel you want to put into action.

8. Describe your plan to implement your solution. (For example, when and where will you put your plan into effect?)

My teacher and I will write my solutions down on a card that I can keep with me in all classrooms.

I can look at this card during the lesson to remember what I need to do. I can complete the

Behavior Contract Scorecard myself and check with my teacher to find out how he thinks I did.

I can try my best to sit still, pay attention, get organized, and follow directions.

9. Note the end result: Did your plan accomplish what you had hoped?

My plan is working so far. I am finding my papers and can remember what Mr. Paradise said

during the lesson. I earned a 95% on my last test!

10. If your plan was successful, reward yourself (by saying to yourself "good job" or "way to go" or by allowing yourself to do something special). If your plan was not successful, return to an earlier step (redefine the problem, change your goal, pick another solution, work on your plan).

If you succeed, how will you reward yourself?

I will tell myself, "Great job, Robert!" and will earn five minutes of computer time after I complete

my work.

HOTSAP Form

Child's name _____ Date _____

Form completed by _____

1. What is your problem?

   _____

   _____

   _____

   _____

2. What is your goal or desired end result?

   _____

   _____

   _____

   _____

3. What are your current feelings (angry, scared, sad, embarrassed, etc.)? _____

   _____

4. How strong are your feelings on a 1 (very weak) to 10 (very strong) scale? _____

5. List as many solutions as you can think of that have a good chance of solving the problem and helping you reach your stated goal.

   _____

   _____

   _____

   _____

   _____

   _____

   _____

   _____

   _____

   _____

From *The Behavior Problems Resource Kit,* © 2010 by Michael J. Asher, Steven B. Gordon, Michael C. Selbst, and Mark Cooperberg, Champaign, IL: Research Press (800-519-2707, www.researchpress.com)

6. Review each solution and decide if it is a good idea, bad idea, and why. Put a plus sign (+) next to the solution if it is a good idea. Put a minus sign (–) next to the solution if it is a bad idea.

7. Circle the solution or solutions you feel you want to put into action.

8. Describe your plan to implement your solution. (For example, when and where will you put your plan into effect?)

_____

_____

_____

_____

_____

9. Note the end result: Did your plan accomplish what you had hoped?

_____

_____

_____

_____

_____

10. If your plan was successful, reward yourself (by saying to yourself "good job" or "way to go" or by allowing yourself to do something special). If your plan was not successful, return to an earlier step (redefine the problem, change your goal, pick another solution, work on your plan).

If you succeed, how will you reward yourself?

_____

_____

_____

_____

_____

3-D Skills Approach:
Discussion, Demonstration, Doing

The 3-D Skills Approach is a set of skills teaching guidelines to help adults collaborate with children and adolescents to design and implement emotional, social, behavioral or functional skills training vignettes that the child can practice on an ongoing basis. The procedure is based generally on the four-part Skillstreaming or structured learning procedure developed by Goldstein and colleagues (Goldstein & McGinnis, 1997): modeling, role playing, performance feedback, and generalization training.

The approach is useful for parents as well as clinicians and teachers. The belief is that each adult working with the child can identify problematic situations and then determine the specific steps necessary to correct the difficulties the child is experiencing. The 3-D procedure begins with a *discussion* of the specific problem impeding social success, followed by a *demonstration* of the socially appropriate behaviors necessary for success. The demonstration is broken down into practical steps that can be rehearsed by the child. Finally, a *doing* procedure is established to ensure opportunities for the skill to be practiced and transferred to the appropriate social setting. Importantly, the technique allows children to learn appropriate behavioral alternatives to unacceptable behaviors.

Some general instructions for using the technique follow:

1. Review the 3-D Skills Approach until the child has memorized the skill steps. Then ask the child to name the skills and describe the steps of the skill several times before a problematic activity or situation begins. (If appropriate, you can help the child write the skills steps on a note card for review.)

2. Rehearsal and role play need to continue beyond the initial discussion, demonstration, and doing phases of instruction. Practice the social-behavioral skill on a daily basis so that it becomes part of the child's behavioral repertoire. Provide plenty of praise and encouragement.

3. Remind the child about the skill periodically and continue giving praise when the child uses the skill.

An outline for a 3-D Approach Group Presentation follows, showing how a teacher or clinician can conduct a group social skills training session. A blank copy of the 3-D Skills Approach Form is provided following two samples of that form—one for home and the other for school. The 3-D Skills Monitoring Form provides a place to list the skill and its steps and to record practice.

Introduction

1. Greet children and develop/review of session rules.

2. Briefly review previous session (review will not occur during the first session).

3. Review activity/assignment from last session.

4. Teacher presents and define a specific skill to be targeted during the session.

5. Teacher provides a specific learning objective.

Discussion

1. Teacher introduces the skill by asking the group questions.

2. To make sure the children understand the skills, the teacher reads the definition of the skill and discusses it with the group.

3. Teacher provides a rationale for the importance of the specific behavior.

4. Teacher outlines steps for doing/performing the behavior.

Demonstration

1. Teacher models the behavior (both correctly and incorrectly).

2. Teacher breaks down the individual major steps for enacting the behavior.

3. Group members engage in role play of a typical situation in which the behavior should be displayed.

4. Teacher leads a discussion of alternative behaviors to accomplish the same goal. (This will help the children develop a repertoire of appropriate behaviors and better understand which behaviors are inappropriate and why.)

Doing

1. Children define the behavior.

2. Children provide a rationale for using the behavior.

3. Children list critical steps for enacting the behavior.

4. Children model the behavior for each other.

5. Children use the behavior in role plays.

6. Teacher asks group members to provide feedback to each other about their role play. Teacher provides feedback for the children about their role play.

Follow-through and practice

1. Teacher provides activities for the children to perform between sessions (i.e., skill homework). These activities will include practicing specific steps that make up each skill. Also, brief parent-child activity sheets will be sent home at the end of each session. This encourages discussion of the skills and fosters skill development.

2. Teacher encourages children to use the learned skill in other settings (home, school, neighborhood)—practicing the skills when they are needed most.

3. During the initial part of the subsequent session, the teacher and children review and briefly practice the social-behavioral skill learned during the previous session.

Feedback to children and parents

1. Teacher completes a monitoring form (rating of child's behavior/participation).

2. Group members report their individual progress and progress of the group.

3. Teacher provides verbal feedback to group.

4. Teacher provides reinforcement.

5. All forms placed in child's folder for parent to review with child at home.

Sample 3-D Skills Approach Form—Home

Child's name _George_   Date _May 28_

SOCIAL-BEHAVIORAL SKILL

Responding appropriately to teasing from peers/siblings

SKILL OBJECTIVE

The child will appropriately respond to teasing or name-calling from peers/siblings.

DISCUSS

This skill is important because:

Sometimes you can get the other person to stop teasing you by ignoring them, changing the

subject, making a joke, or complimenting the other person.

Specific skill steps:

1. Decide whether or not you are being teased.

2. Try to understand why you are being teased.

3. Choose a specific strategy if you are being teased to try to get the teaser to stop:

    a. ignore the other person.

    b. make a joke.

    c. compliment the other person to show maturity.

    d. change the subject.

4. Act out your best choice.

5. Evaluate how you did and how the teaser reacted.

Please complete the following:

Other people we know who are good at this skill are:

My friend John—he laughs along with whatever others say. He acts like it's not a big deal.

Other people who are not so good are:

This guy Peter in my scout troop. He gets mad even if people aren't talking directly to him. He thinks

he is always being teased. The other scouts avoid him.

How would life be better if you were good at this skill?

If I could make a choice not to respond to being teased I wouldn't get so angry. I think I would feel

better and get along better.

Situations that are relevant for this skill are:

The places I could use this are at home with my brother and sister, on the playground, at scouts,

and at soccer.

DEMONSTRATE

1. Demonstrate the skill for your child, identifying the correct steps.

2. Next, demonstrate the wrong way to use the skill, purposely leaving steps out.

3. Identify the missing steps.

DO

Please follow the steps below and keep a record of practice:

1. Ask your child to name the skill to be worked on.

2. Ask your child to tell you why the skill is important.

3. Ask your child to tell you (or read) the steps of the skills.

4. Have your child do the steps in a role-play situation.

5. Use coaching and feedback to fine tune the target skill. Smiling and verbal praise (e.g., That's right! I like the way you did/said that. You did a great job!) are very important.

Sample 3-D Skills Approach–Home (page 2 of 2)

Sample 3-D Skills Approach Form—School

Child's name ___Miranda_____ Date ___September 17_____

SOCIAL-BEHAVIORAL SKILL

_Controlling temper in conflict situations with adults/peers_____

SKILL OBJECTIVE

The child will control her temper in conflict situations with others. Child will learn more effective/

_mature ways to deal with her anger._____

DISCUSS

This skill is important because:

You can sometimes get others to hear your side if you can control your temper, if you disagree with

others in a nice manner, they will sometimes change their position or better understand your feelings;

most times, losing your temper with adults is a "no-win" situation for you; you can often reach an

_agreement with an adult by calmly presenting your side._____

Specific skill steps:

1. Stop and count to 10 (allow yourself 10 seconds to cool off and think). During the 10 seconds,

_____focus on breathing slowly._____

_2. Think about your choices:_____

_____a. I could tell the person in calm words why I am angry._____

_____b. I could walk away for now._____

_____c. I could find a good time to talk to the person about the problem._____

_____d. I could write about how I feel._____

_____e. I could do a relaxation exercise._____

Please complete the following:

Other people we know who are good at this skill are:

My Uncle Joe is good at controlling his temper. He told me that he used to get really mad and that he didn't like the way he acted and the way it made him feel. He said that he decided that he would learn to control his temper and not get so mad.

Other people who are not so good are:

My dad gets really angry with me, my brother and sister, and my mom. He scares us, so we try not to make him mad.

How would life be better if you were good at this skill?

My friends look upset when I get mad. If I could control my temper, I think they would want to be around me more.

Situations that are relevant for this skill are:

I could work on controlling my temper when I'm with my friends, with my family, and when I have a hard time with my schoolwork. I really need to control myself when I play sports, too.

DEMONSTRATE

1. Demonstrate the skill for your child, identifying the correct steps.
2. Next, demonstrate the wrong way to use the skill, purposely leaving steps out.
3. Identify the missing steps.

DO

Please follow the steps below and keep a record of practice:

1. Ask your child to name the skill to be worked on.
2. Ask your child to tell you why the skill is important.
3. Ask your child to tell you (or read) the steps of the skills.
4. Have your child do the steps in a role-play situation.
5. Use coaching and feedback to fine tune the target skill. Smiling and verbal praise (e.g., That's right! I like the way you did/said that. You did a great job!) are very important.

Sample 3-D Skills Approach–School (page 2 of 2)

3-D Skills Approach Form

Child's name _____ Date _____

SOCIAL-BEHAVIORAL SKILL

_____

SKILL OBJECTIVE

_____

_____

DISCUSS

This skill is important because:

_____

_____

_____

_____

_____

Specific skill steps:

_____

_____

_____

_____

_____

_____

_____

_____

_____

_____

_____

Please complete the following:

Other people we know who are good at this skill are:

_____

_____

_____

Other people who are not so good are:

_____

_____

_____

How would life be better if you were good at this skill?

_____

_____

_____

Situations that are relevant for this skill are:

_____

_____

_____

DEMONSTRATE

1. Demonstrate the skill for your child, identifying the correct steps.

2. Next, demonstrate the wrong way to use the skill, purposely leaving steps out.

3. Identify the missing steps.

DO

Please follow the steps below and keep a record of practice:

1. Ask your child to name the skill to be worked on.

2. Ask your child to tell you why the skill is important.

3. Ask your child to tell you (or read) the steps of the skills.

4. Have your child do the steps in a role-play situation.

5. Use coaching and feedback to fine tune the target skill. Smiling and verbal praise (e.g., That's right! I like the way you did/said that. You did a great job!) are very important.

3-D Skills Approach Monitoring Form

Child's name _____ Date _____

Form completed by _____

3-D skill to be practiced _____

Identified steps of the skill:

Step 1. _____

Step 2. _____

Step 3. _____

Step 4. _____

Step 5. _____

Specific locations skill should be practiced: _____

_____

Specific people skill will be practiced with: _____

_____

Specific examples of skill situations: _____

_____

Week 1

Monday	☐	☐	☐	☐	☐	☐
Tuesday	☐	☐	☐	☐	☐	☐
Wednesday	☐	☐	☐	☐	☐	☐
Thursday	☐	☐	☐	☐	☐	☐
Friday	☐	☐	☐	☐	☐	☐
Saturday	☐	☐	☐	☐	☐	☐
Sunday	☐	☐	☐	☐	☐	☐

Week 2

Monday	☐	☐	☐	☐	☐	☐
Tuesday	☐	☐	☐	☐	☐	☐
Wednesday	☐	☐	☐	☐	☐	☐
Thursday	☐	☐	☐	☐	☐	☐
Friday	☐	☐	☐	☐	☐	☐
Saturday	☐	☐	☐	☐	☐	☐
Sunday	☐	☐	☐	☐	☐	☐

Social Scripting

Social scripting, or self-instruction, was originally developed by Daniel Meichenbaum for children with attention deficit/hyperactivity disorder (AD/HD) and has been used for children with pervasive developmental disorders, and those with severe psychiatric disorders. Individuals with many differing disorders may also show performance deficiencies in social and performance situations due to failure to attend to subtle social cues and be aware of solutions and rules that may govern their actions. Social scripting may help to address these problems, especially for younger children.

Social scripts should be written collaboratively with the adult. They involve three types of sentences:

1. Problem identification provides basic information about the problems the child is facing.

2. Social-emotional-behavioral goals or solutions direct the form the behavior should take.

3. Positive self-statements provide information about the feelings of self and/or others.

Creativity is an asset in using the social scripting approach, as is experimentation with regard to frequency and timing of story generation. It can be helpful to have children fill out the Social Scripting Handout before writing their own scripts. The Social Scripting Form provides a structure to assist children in coming up with their own stories.

The following two sample scripts illustrate the type of information included.

SCRIPT 1: STAYING CALM WHEN THE FIRE ALARM RINGS

1. I have a problem when the fire alarm rings. When the alarm rings, it can be loud and sometimes hurts my ears. I feel scared of the loud noise.

2. My goal is to leave the building with my class so that we can stay safe. Now I know that I can take deep breaths, stay calm, and leave the school with my friends.

3. When I do this, my teachers and I will be happy and safe. I did a good job.

SCRIPT 2: HOW TO GET ALONG

1. Sometimes I get annoyed and bothered by other people. I can get pretty annoyed.

2. I know it is important not to let others bother me. I need to try to be pleasant and get along. I could negotiate how to spend time and share space.

3. If I can be more pleasant, I can tell myself how well I did to get along. I could also feel good about how nice I acted and how I was able to make someone else feel okay.

Social Scripting Handout

Child's name _____ Date _____

Form completed by _____

Identified problem

☐ Somebody teased me.   ☐ I was scared of something
☐ Somebody took something of mine.   ☐ Something bothered me.
☐ Somebody told me to do something.   ☐ Others didn't play fair.
☐ Somebody was doing something I didn't like. ☐ I didn't get something I wanted.
☐ Somebody started fighting with me.   ☐ I didn't win.
☐ I want to be first   ☐ Other _____

How it made me feel

☐ Happy   ☐ Sad   ☐ Scared   ☐ Embarrassed   ☐ Mad

How strong was this feeling? (circle best choice)

1	2	3	4	5	6	7	8	9	10
Weak				Medium					Strong

My goals and solutions are to . . . (choose one from each column—an emotional, social, and behavioral goal)

Emotional	Social	Behavioral
☐ control my anger	☐ give compliments	☐ follow the rules
☐ not be scared	☐ be assertive with others	☐ wait my turn
☐ be happy	☐ talk it out calmly	☐ do something else
☐ not let things bother me	☐ get along with others	☐ work out a plan
☐ handle disappointment	☐ ignore	☐ switch to a new activity
☐ other _____	☐ other _____	☐ other _____

When I succeed at handling my problems, what do I say to myself?

☐ I did a good job.   ☐ My mother or father is proud of me.
☐ I controlled myself.   ☐ My teacher is happy about my work.
☐ I behaved well.   ☐ other _____
☐ I got along well with others. ☐ other _____

From *The Behavior Problems Resource Kit,* © 2010 by Michael J. Asher, Steven B. Gordon, Michael C. Selbst, and Mark Cooperberg, Champaign, IL: Research Press (800-519-2707, www.researchpress.com)

Social Scripting Form

Child's name _____ Date _____

Form completed by _____

1. Identified problem

   _____

   _____

   _____

   _____

   _____

2. My emotional, social, and behavioral goals and solutions

   _____

   _____

   _____

   _____

   _____

3. When I succeed at handling my problems, what do I say to myself?

   _____

   _____

   _____

   _____

   _____

Social Skills Contract

Children and adolescents who demonstrate behavior difficulties often have deficient social skills and may require direct instruction in these skills to function effectively in social situations. The Social Skills Contract is an agreement between a child and supervising adult designed to encourage the child to work on a particular social skill. It specifies the steps in the skill as well as the adult's responsibilities in helping the child use and master the skill. A sample contract follows, along with a reproducible Social Skills Contract Form.

Some helpful skills and their steps include the following.

Listening and Following Directions

1. Look at Mom when she is talking.

2. Listen carefully to the directions.

3. Repeat the directions to yourself.

4. If you don't know how to begin, ask a question.

5. Check yourself to see if you are following the steps.

Being a Good Sport If Losing

1. Remain calm and continue to play.

2. Talk to others in a quiet voice.

3. Compliment whoever is winning.

4. Encourage other players.

5. Continue to be cooperative.

Giving a Compliment

1. Look for things others do that you can compliment.

2. Tell the person what you like.

3. Pat the person on the back or give a high-five.

4. Stay with the activity and keep looking for behaviors to compliment.

Going Along with Another Person's Idea

1. Listen carefully to the idea.

2. Think of what is good about the idea.

3. Praise the person for what you think is good.

4. Go along with the idea.

5. Keep your idea to yourself until you are asked to share it.

Sample Social Skills Contract

Child's name ____Carson_____ Date ____January 10____

I agree to work very hard at improving my social skills. The name of the specific skill I will be practicing is:

_Staying calm when I am frustrated._____

The steps of this skill are:

1. Notice that I am getting upset and angry.

2. Tell myself to "Get Calm Right Now."

3. Take five slow, deep breaths, breathing in

   through my nose (like smelling pizza) and out

   through my mouth (blowing out candles).

4. Find a safe place to sit down.

5. Think of my solutions by using HOTSAP.

6. If I forget HOTSAP, tell an adult that I need help.

Adult's name ____Ms. Freedman_____ Date ____January 10____

My job will be to:

1. Meet with Carson and review the contract in the morning, before lunch, and at the end of the day.

2. Provide encouragement in the form of praise.

3. Go over to Carson when he starts to get upset and encourage him to discuss the problem.

I did my job on these dates:

Date	Adult's initials
1/19	BF
1/20	BF
1/21	BF
1/22	BF

Social Skills Contract Form

Child's name _____ Date _____

I agree to work very hard at improving my social skills. The name of the specific skill I will be practicing is:

_____

The steps of this skill are:

_____

_____

_____

_____

_____

Adult's name _____ Date _____

My job will be to:

_____

_____

_____

_____

_____

_____

I did my job on these dates:

Date	Adult's initials
_____	_____
_____	_____
_____	_____
_____	_____
_____	_____

From *The Behavior Problems Resource Kit,* © 2010 by Michael J. Asher, Steven B. Gordon, Michael C. Selbst, and Mark Cooperberg, Champaign, IL: Research Press (800-519-2707, www.researchpress.com)

Cue and Review

Cue and Review helps children and adolescents plan for demanding situations (i.e., those situations that pose difficulties on a fairly regular and predictable basis). Once these situations are identified, a task analysis is undertaken to break the larger task down into its component parts. These parts are most commonly arranged sequentially (i.e., first you do . . . then you do . . . followed by . . .). Then a time is chosen to review these steps. The steps are always presented immediately before the high-risk situation (Cue) and may be reviewed as many times as desired after the situation (Review).

The steps may be prepared in picture form for younger children (three through seven) and in written form for older children (eight through twelve). Some younger children may do well with written statements; some older children may require pictures.

Cue and Review focuses on gradually shifting responsibility for the steps from the supervising adult (parent or teacher) to the child. This is best done through the use of questioning (e.g., "What's the first thing you do when you come into the class from recess?"). Next the adult carefully monitors the performance of each step, providing feedback and allowing the child to review his or her performance, effectively prompting the child to learn self-monitoring and self-evaluation skills. These self-monitoring and self-evaluation skills are critical components of self-control.

Virtually anything that happens can be broken down into steps and taught by using Cue and Review. Following is a sample dialogue between a father and son, illustrating the type of interaction that takes place between adult and child during Cue and Review. The Cue and Review Card resulting from that dialogue is included. The remainder of this section presents a number of common high-risk situations at home and at school, broken down into their component steps.

SAMPLE DIALOGUE

In the following dialogue, a father and a seven-year-old son are discussing the dinner hour, a high-risk situation for the son because his older sister often interrupts him when he's telling a story about his day. The son becomes frustrated and angry and yells at or hits his sister, resulting in his being sent away from the table. His parents estimate this occurs during 75 percent of the meals they have together. The son has acknowledged that this is a problem, and the father is developing a Cue and Review plan.

Father: So, what are the things you need to do at dinner so you don't get sent from the table?

Son: *(Shrugs his shoulders.)* I don't know.

Father: What if you use pleasant talk?

Son: Uh-huh.

Father: What if you keep your hands to yourself?

Son: Sure.

Father: Finally, what if, when your sister interrupts you or teases you or does something annoying, you make a "T-sign" with your hands—you know, like the refs do at your basketball games when they call for time-out, except we'll know it stands for a tease by your sister? This way your mom and I will know you are upset, and we will take care of it so you won't have to lose your cool and get into trouble. How does that sound?

Son: OK, I guess.

Father: Well, let's look at those three steps. First, pleasant talk. Second, keep hands to yourself, and, third, make the T-sign when your sister teases you, and we will handle it. Here's a card to remind you of what you need to do at dinner. I'll go over this with you privately before we sit down, and then I'll go over it again with you privately after dinner.

Sample Cue and Review Card

Dinner Time

1. Pleasant talk.

2. Keep hands to self.

3. Make T-sign when sister teases.

HIGH-RISK HOME SITUATIONS

Parents can choose from the following situations and adapt the steps to their own circumstances. They can analyze and break down other situations as the need presents: visiting someone else's house, riding in the car, bath time, going to the store/public places, playing alone, playing with other children, watching TV, having company at the house, going to a place of worship, doing household chores, having conversations with adults/others.

Getting Up

1. Wake up.
2. Get out of bed.
3. Head for the bathroom.

Morning Wash Up

1. Brush teeth.
2. Wash face and hands.
3. Return to bedroom.
4. Get dressed.

Breakfast

1. Sit at kitchen table.
2. Eat breakfast.
3. Put dishes in sink.

Coming Home after School

1. Walk into house.
2. Say hello to parent.
3. Remove and hang up coat.
4. Have a snack.

Getting Ready for Homework

1. Unpack book bag.
2. Take out homework folder and put on desk.
3. Think about what homework I have to do.
4. Estimate time for each assignment.

Doing Homework

1. Read directions.
2. Sit quietly at desk.
3. Put name on paper.
4. Complete work.
5. Put homework back in folder.
6. Repack bookbag.

Free Time

1. Choose activity.
2. Play quietly.
3. Wait for directions.

Book Bag Check

1. Put homework papers in homework folder.
2. Pack lunch.
3. Pack other materials.
4. Zip backpack.

Getting Out the Door

1. Put on hat and coat.

2. Put book bag on back.

3. Kiss good-bye.

Riding the School Bus

1. Line up at bus stop.

2. Get into the bus.

3. Sit in a seat.

4. Listen to and follow bus driver's directions.

Getting Ready for Dinner

1. Wash hands.

2. Sit at the table.

3. Talk with family.

4. Ask to be excused when finished eating.

5. Put dishes in sink.

Relaxing before Bedtime

1. Choose activity.

2. Sit and/or play quietly.

3. Ask for snack.

4. Clean up.

5. Wait for directions.

Getting Ready for Bed

1. Get pajamas.

2. Go to bathroom

3. Brush teeth.

4. Take bath or shower.

5. Return to bedroom.

Bedtime

1. Choose book to read.

2. Read quietly with parent.

3. Read quietly to myself.

4. Turn out lights and say good night.

5. Turn on radio.

6. Remain quietly in bed.

HIGH-RISK SCHOOL SITUATIONS

Teachers will need to choose from among the following situations and adapt the steps to suit their own circumstances. In addition, they can analyze and break down other times and situations as the need presents: working in small groups, when the teacher is talking and giving directions, lining up, walking down school hallways, when in the bathroom, when on field trips, during special assemblies, at recess, when talking to others.

Starting the Day

1. Hang up coat.
2. Unpack book bag at desk.
3. Place homework folder on desk.
4. Put lunch box in closet.
5. Put book bag in pile in front of closet.
6. Return to seat and begin work.

Independent Seatwork

1. Listen to directions.
2. Stay in seat.
3. Work quietly on assignment.
4. Raise hand and wait in seat for help.

Finishing Up in the Morning

1. Put name on all papers.
2. Pass papers in as teacher says.

Free Time

1. Keep hands and feet to myself.
2. Play quietly.

Getting Ready for Lunch

1. Wash hands.
2. Get lunch box.
3. Sit down at desk.
4. Walk in line when called.

Lunch Time

1. Walk quietly in line.
2. Talk quietly with classmates.
3. Keep hands and feet to myself.

Indoor Recess

1. Share toys and materials with classmates.
2. Clean up when told.
3. Sit down when told.

Completing Assignments

1. Listen to directions.
2. Repeat directions.
3. Complete the assignment.

Going to Another Class

1. Walk quietly in line.
2. Listen and follow directions.
3. Keep hands and feet to yourself.

Listening

1. Sit quietly.
2. Look at the teacher.
3. Think about what the teacher is saying.

Library Time

1. Sit down quietly at the table.
2. Find books when told.
3. Sign books out.
4. Sit down and read books quietly.

Going Home

1. Put papers inside homework folder.
2. Find books and other materials.
3. Get book bag and pack it up.
4. Get coat and put it on.
5. Wait at desk for instructions.

CONSEQUENCE INTERVENTIONS: CONTROLLING POSITIVE AND NEGATIVE REINFORCEMENT

- Home Environment Learning Program (HELP) (p. 187)
    Sample HELP Reward Menu
    Sample HELP Weekly Record Form
    HELP Behavior Rating Scale
    HELP Reward Menu
    HELP Weekly Record Form

Behavior Contracts

Behavior contracts address common problems that result from people's different perceptions and memories. By putting in writing agreements between the child and adult, problems are greatly minimized. A Class Behavior Contract for the elementary level follows, illustrating clear expectations/rules, reasons for for following them, positive consequences, and negative consequences. Space is provided for student, parent, and teacher to sign. A Sample Behavior Contract is next included, followed by a blank Behavior Contract Form. Finally, the Behavior Contract Scorecard allows both child and adult to enable them to become more aware of positive behaviors and in turn improve relationships.

EXPECTATIONS/RULES

All students will:

1. Show respect for the teacher and other students by

    a. remaining quiet when others are talking.

    b. listening when others are talking.

    c. either making positive comments about others or saying nothing.

    d. keeping hands and feet to themselves.

    e. remaining safe with all materials and furniture.

    f. respecting personal space (stay at least an arm's length away from others).

2. Raise hand and wait to be called upon before speaking.

3. Speak in class

    a. using an inside voice (no shouting).

    b. sharing only information about the topic.

    c. using appropriate language at all times (no cursing or name-calling).

4. Remain seated on chair and feet on the floor.

5. Arrive on time to class.

6. Complete assigned work to the best of their ability.

7. Ask for help from the teacher when needed.

8. Calmly and quietly discuss any concerns or problems.

REASON/RATIONALE FOR FOLLOWING EXPECTATIONS/RULES

Following these expectations and rules will:

1. Maintain safety in the class and school.

2. Allow for students to learn.

3. Allow for teachers to teach.

4. Help students to get along better with each other and with staff members.

POSITIVE CONSEQUENCES

When students follow the rules, they will:

1. Receive praise from staff members.

2. Have the greatest opportunity to learn.

3. Have an easier time with homework.

4. Receive a free homework pass for any one class in which they follow all rules for five days.

   a. These do not need to be five days in a row.

   b. Students may earn a homework pass for each subject.

   c. Teachers keep track of those students who follow all the rules each day.

NEGATIVE CONSEQUENCES

When a student does not follow a rule as stated in this contract, the following consequences will be implemented:

1. Minor misbehaviors will be ignored, provided they do not disrupt the classroom lesson.

2. If the behavior continues and/or becomes disruptive, the student will be reminded of the violation of the classroom rule and that the next time there is any rule violation today, it will result in a Sit and Watch procedure (p. 103).

3. The next time there is any rule violation the same day, the student will be required to move away from the other students and sit in the Sit and Watch chair.

Sit and Watch

1. Once the student sits in this area, the teacher informs the student of the rule that was violated and asks the student to repeat it.

2. The teacher informs the student of the need to sit and watch how the other students follow the rule.

3. While the student watches, the teacher makes a point of praising other students for rule compliance.

4. After three minutes of the student remaining calm, the adult approaches the student and asks the student to state the rule that was violated and what should be done instead.

5. Then the student returns to the activity if the response is appropriate.

6. When the student returns to the activity, the teacher provides behavior-specific praise for rule compliance (e.g., "John, I like the way you are raising your hand quietly").

7. If the behavior escalates or continues the same day, the teacher should implement a second Sit and Watch procedure.

8. If the behavior then escalates or continues the same day, the student is sent to the principal's office and a detention is given. A call to the parent/guardian is made as well.

9. After two detentions, a parent/guardian and teacher conference is arranged.

Class Behavior Contract (page 2 of 3)

I have read and agree to the above contract. I have asked any questions I have regarding this contract.

_____   _____
Student name (print)   Date

_____
Student signature

_____   _____
Parent/guardian name (print)   Date

_____
Parent/guardian signature

_____   _____
Teacher name (print)   Date

_____
Teacher signature

Sample Behavior Contract

Child's name ___Kenisha_____ Date ___September 22_____

Form completed by ___Mr. Paradise_____

This behavior contract is entered into by both parties with the understanding that its goal is to produce an improvement in school and/or at home. Both parties agree to put forth their best effort.

___Kenisha_____ agrees to:

1. ___Be prepared each day for Mr. Paradise's English class._____

2. ___Participate and complete assigned class work._____

3. ___Interact appropriately with fellow classmates._____

4. ___Complete all assigned homework._____

5. ___Follow classroom rules as posted._____

Signature ___Kenisha_____

_____ agrees to:

1. ___Provide Kenisha with check-in and check-out assistance at the beginning and end of class.___

2. ___Modify assignments, allowing Kenisha a chance to complete assigned work.___

3. ___Grade Kenisha on participation and work completion, providing one point each day toward her final grade.___

4. ___Meet with Kenisha weekly to review progress and establish a plan for the coming week.___

5. _____

Signature ___Mr. Paradise_____

Child's name _____ Date _____

Form completed by _____

This behavior contract is entered into by both parties with the understanding that its goal is to produce an improvement in school and/or at home. Both parties agree to put forth their best effort.

_____ agrees to:

1. _____

2. _____

3. _____

4. _____

5. _____

Signature _____

_____ agrees to:

1. _____

2. _____

3. _____

4. _____

5. _____

Signature _____

From *The Behavior Problems Resource Kit,* © 2010 by Michael J. Asher, Steven B. Gordon, Michael C. Selbst, and Mark Cooperberg, Champaign, IL: Research Press (800-519-2707, www.researchpress.com)

Please keep score of your own behavior. If you adhered to all the terms of the contract for the day, please enter a "yes" in the appropriate box. If you did not adhere to all the terms of the contract, please enter a "no" in the apppropriate box.

Contract for (child's name) _____ Date _____

	Monday	Tuesday	Wednesday	Thursday	Friday	Saturday	Sunday
1							
2							
3							
4							
5							

Daily Behavior Report Card

The Daily Behavior Report Card is an effective behavioral strategy to incorporate into the child's behavior intervention plan. The report card typically includes having the student's teacher or paraprofessional rate the child on one or more specific behaviors. It is often desirable (and more effective) to rate each behavior at the end of each period, subject, or major transition time (i.e., about seven or eight times a day) for each of the behaviors. Behaviors may include items such as "Remained quiet when teacher/others were talking," "Raised hand to ask or answer questions or make a comment," and "Kept his hands and feet to himself." These replacement behaviors help the child and coach (i.e., teacher, paraprofessional, parent) to maintain greater focus on developing and reinforcing the desired behavior than on attending to the target behavior.

The adult may rate the child's behavior via a three-point Likert scale (0 = not true at all, 1 = somewhat or sometimes true, 3 = mostly or completely true), recording this at the end of the time period. Feedback is given to the child, including behavior-specific praise, constructive criticism when appropriate, and a "star" sticker (for example) to place on a chart. A reward tower may also be used, consisting of a pre-made tower of blocks printed on a piece of paper. The child places the star sticker on the lowest block first, then the one above that, and so on. The child can then watch as stars are accumulated, working toward the criterion set. Sometimes, a morning criterion and afternoon criterion are used with one reward tower for each part of the day, so that the child has a chance to earn up to two rewards per day. The number of blocks can be gradually increased based upon the child's progress.

It is recommended that a baseline score be gathered for about seven days to assist in determining a reasonable daily criterion for the child to achieve. The child should be unaware of the Daily Behavior Report Card, and there should be no rewards presented during this time period. The determined criterion should then remain constant for about two weeks. The goal needs to be realistic and relatively easy to reach initially. Every several weeks, the goal may be gradually increased. The child should be actively involved in the discussion of rewards and made aware of the target behaviors and required point totals (after baseline has been gathered). A reward menu like the one in Appendix A may be used to list various possible rewards. The coach may also write brief comments on the bottom of the report card and sign and date the form.

A copy of the specific, desired behavior(s) can be placed on the child's desk. This can be in the form of a checklist to self-monitor behavior by checking each item after it is completed for each period. It is typically necessary to teach the desired skills and have the child practice them frequently at set times. If desired, the report card may include pictures of the behavior to provide the student with visual cues.

Two sample Daily Behavior Report Cards follow—one for an elementary age child and the other for a middle/high school age student. A generic blank form is also provided. Use these forms as models for creating individualized report cards to address each child's particular needs.

Sample Daily Behavior Report Card—Elementary School

Student's name ___Marcus___ Date ___November 20___

*Directions Please write in the activity or class in the first row of the chart
(e.g., 1 = reading; 2 = math; 3 = spelling; 4 = lunch)*

Behavior	Class/ activity 1	Class/ activity 2	Class/ activity 3	Class/ activity 4	Class/ activity 5	Class/ activity 6	Class/ activity 7	Class/ activity 8
1. Maintained inside/ quiet voice.	⓪ 1 2	0 ① 2	0 ① 2	0 ① 2	0 ① 2	0 ① 2	0 ① 2	⓪ 1 2
2. Maintained appropriate self-control and stayed calm (kept body to myself, appropriate with materials, remained in class unless given permission, used feelings words if needed)	⓪ 1 2	0 ① 2	0 ① 2	0 ① 2	0 ① 2	0 ① 2	⓪ 1 2	⓪ 1 2
3. Completed assigned class work (0 =< 33%; 1 = 33–67%; 2 =>67%)	⓪ 1 2	⓪ 1 2	0 ① 2	0 ① 2	0 ① 2	0 ① 2	⓪ 1 2	⓪ 1 2
I earn a sticker when I get two points for each behavior			🙂	🙂	🙂	🙂		
Total number of points earned for the day (add total from bottom of each column)	Total 3	Total 5	Total 6	Total 6	Total 6	Total 6	Total 4	Total 2

Total points earned: ___44___

0 = not at all true   1 = somewhat or sometimes true   2 = mostly or completely true

Number of points needed to earn award: ___40___

Comments ___Struggled at start and end of day. Most difficulty centered on written work. Got upset when asked to correct work.___

Staff signature ___Ms. Biggs___

Sample Daily Behavior Report Card—Middle/High School

Student's name ___Emily___   Date ___September 24___

Behavior	Class Period 1	Class Period 2	Class Period 3	Class Period 4
1. Student completed all homework assignments.	☑ Yes (2) ☐ No (0) Comments:	☐ Yes (2) ☑ No (0) Comments: *missing p. 20*	☑ Yes (2) ☐ No (0) Comments:	☑ Yes (2) ☐ No (0) Comments:
2. Student completed all class assignments.	☑ Yes (2) ☐ No (0) Comments:	☑ Yes (2) ☐ No (0) Comments:	☑ Yes (2) ☐ No (0) Comments:	☑ Yes (2) ☐ No (0) Comments:
3. Student followed rules and was respectful.	☑ Yes (2) ☐ No (0) Comments:	☑ Yes (2) ☐ No (0) Comments:	☑ Yes (2) ☐ No (0) Comments:	☑ Yes (2) ☐ No (0) Comments:
4. Student maintained self-control.	☑ Yes (2) ☐ No (0) Comments:	☑ Yes (2) ☐ No (0) Comments:	☑ Yes (2) ☐ No (0) Comments:	☑ Yes (2) ☐ No (0) Comments:
5. Student socialized adequately with peers.	☐ Yes (2) ☑ No (0) Comments: *did not speak*	☐ Yes (2) ☑ No (0) Comments:	☑ Yes (2) ☑ No (0) Comments:	☑ Yes (2) ☐ No (0) Comments: *worked well with partner*
Bonus Points (giving compliments, ignoring teasing)	Circle each bonus point 1 1 1	Circle each bonus point ① 1 1	Circle each bonus point 1 1 1	Circle each bonus point 1 1 1
Totals	8	7	8	10

Teacher's name ___Mrs. Lutz___   Total points earned ___33___

Comments ___Great job working with partner during fourth period. Seemed to enjoy developing creative story about television show.___

Daily Behavior Report Card Form

Student's name _____ Date _____

Note the activity/class below the number (e.g., 1 = reading, 2 = math, 3 = spelling, 4 = lunch).

Behavior	Activity 1	Activity 2	Activity 3	Activity 4	Activity 5	Activity 6	Activity 7
1.	0 1 2 n/a	0 1 2 n/a	0 1 2 n/a	0 1 2 n/a	0 1 2 n/a	0 1 2 n/a	0 1 2 n/a
2.	0 1 2 n/a	0 1 2 n/a	0 1 2 n/a	0 1 2 n/a	0 1 2 n/a	0 1 2 n/a	0 1 2 n/a
3.	0 1 2 n/a	0 1 2 n/a	0 1 2 n/a	0 1 2 n/a	0 1 2 n/a	0 1 2 n/a	0 1 2 n/a
4.	0 1 2 n/a	0 1 2 n/a	0 1 2 n/a	0 1 2 n/a	0 1 2 n/a	0 1 2 n/a	0 1 2 n/a
Total points for the day _____	Total _____	Total _____	Total _____	Total _____	Total _____	Total _____	Total _____

Points Rating: 0 = not at all   1 = somewhat or sometimes true   2 = mostly or completely true   **Number of points needed to earn reward:** _____

Comments _____

Staff name _____ Staff signature _____

Stop and Think Planning Essay

The Stop and Think Planning Essay helps the adult develop a point of cognitive mediation for a child or adolescent who has committed a behavioral infraction. At the conclusion of any rule violation, the child completes this form, which is an opportunity to turn a negative situation into a learning experience. The adult encourages the child to respond to the guiding questions in a comprehensive manner. Two sample Stop and Think Essays, one for home and one for school, are followed by a blank Stop and Think Essay Form.

Sample Stop and Think Planning Essay–Home

Child's name _____ Max _____ Date _____ April 3 _____

Form completed by _____ Max and Dr. Asher _____

1. What I did that got me into trouble was:

   I got into a fight with my sister.

2. Three bad things that happened as a result were:

   My mom got mad and yelled at me.
   I was sent to my room.
   My mom took my DS game.

3. What I should have done instead was:

   I should have told myself that my sister's behavior is not a big deal and then walked away.

4. Three good things that would have happened as a result would be:

   My mom wouldn't have yelled.
   I wouldn't have had to go to my room.
   I would have been able to keep my DS.

5. Please write a description of your plan to prevent the above problems in the future.

   In the future I will try not to get so mad at my sister's behavior and tell myself that whatever she is doing is not a big deal. I will tell myself that I need to walk away and think, I don't need to "sweat the small stuff."

Sample Stop and Think Planning Essay–School

Child's name _____Jonny_____ Date _____March 27_____

Form completed by _____Jonny and Mrs. Paradise_____

1. What I did that got me into trouble was:

   I wasted time and didn't do my classwork.

2. Three bad things that happened as a result were:

   I had to stay in during part of recess and do my work.
   My teacher was disappointed with me.
   I have to write this essay before I go to recess.

3. What I should have done instead was:

   To do my work when my teacher assigned it.

4. Three good things that would have happened as a result would be:

   I would have gone to recess with my class.
   My teacher would have been happy with me.
   I would get my work done faster.

5. Please write a description of your plan to prevent the above problems in the future.

   When I have work to do I will do it when my teacher tells me to. If I have trouble I will ask for help. If I
   can do that I will get my work done and move to new activities with my class.

174

Stop and Think Planning Essay Form

Child's name _____ Date _____

Form completed by _____

1. What I did that got me into trouble was:

2. Three bad things that happened as a result were:

3. What I should have done instead was:

4. Three good things that would have happened as a result would be:

5. Please write a description of your plan to prevent the above problems in the future.

School Environment Learning Program (SELP)

The School Environment Learning Program (SELP) is a highly structured approach often referred to as a point system. It has proven successful in helping teachers, parents, and mental health professionals establish more positive classroom behaviors for children with a wide range of challenging behaviors, classifications and diagnoses. Specifically, this program begins by establishing a preintervention assessment (i.e., baseline) of four essential classroom behaviors:

- following class rules
- completing class work or participating in class (whichever is appropriate)
- completing homework
- getting along with other students

The program then makes use of contingent school and/or home consequences to improve behavior in these four areas.

SELP requires an active collaboration between school personnel. Although the program may seem a bit complicated initially, it is easily understood once put into effect. Significant success is likely in any setting where the participants take the time to implement SELP. However, the program needs to be conducted as written to ensure its integrity, as modifications may decrease effectiveness. By conducting the program as written, teachers, parents, and students experience the benefits of improved academic and social behaviors.

The information presented in the Summary of SELP Rules describes program rules as well as how to use all necessary forms:

- SELP Behavior Rating Scale
- SELP Daily Scorecard
- SELP Reward Menu for Home/School Privileges
- SELP Weekly Record Form

Samples of the last three forms are included for a case example illustrating SELP; reproducible forms appear at the end of this section.

SUMMARY OF SELP RULES

1. Each school day of the week is divided into time periods. These time periods can be times of day (e.g., 9:00–9:30, 9:31–10:00, etc.), or they can correspond to specific academic periods (e.g., reading group, arithmetic, etc.).

2. After each period, the teacher uses the SELP Behavior Rating Scale to assess the student on four target behaviors: follows class rules, completes class work or participates in class (whichever is appropriate), completes homework, and gets along with other students.

3. Ratings of 10, 5, or 0 are entered on the SELP Daily Scorecard. If a behavior category does not apply, the period is marked with an *X*.

4. Initial scoring is done privately for five days, without informing the student, in order to establish a pretreatment baseline or "behavioral X-ray." This is done to ensure that the program begins at the student's correct level of performance rather than at a level based on unrealistic expectations.

5. Teachers and/or parents establish basic privileges at school and/or at home. These privileges consist of approximately four activities that are significant to the child and that can be controlled (e.g., use of TV for the day, going outside, bedtime, recess, free time in class, computer time, etc.).

6. The student needs a predetermined number of points in order to obtain basic privileges. The number of points required is set at approximately 10 percent above the baseline. For example, if the baseline average is 50 points per day, then the number of points to earn basic privileges is 55 points per day.

7. At the end of each school day the teacher and/or parent, with the student's assistance, enters the total number of points earned that day and then informs the student whether or not basic privileges have been earned. These basic privileges will be available during the remainder of the day at home or at school the following day.

8. At the end of each day, the student has an opportunity to discuss performance to address areas of deficiency. This meeting includes feedback about the ratings and plans to address what steps the student can take to improve/maintain the ratings for the next day.

9. All points earned must be used for basic privileges whether the child wants them or not. This means that the child cannot decide to forego spending points for basic privileges in order to deposit them into savings and thereby use them to purchase special privileges.

10. If the student earns more points than needed for basic privileges during any given day, then these extra points are deposited into savings and can be used to purchase special privileges.

11. Special privileges are arranged in advance and posted on the SELP Reward Menu (e.g., homework pass = 40 points, extra time on the classroom computer = 20 points, extra gym time = 50 points).

12. If the student fails to earn the points needed for basic privileges, then the points earned that day are automatically lost. This does not apply to those points already in savings.

13. If privileges are occurring only in school, then points in savings can be used to purchase special privileges only when basic privileges have been earned for two consecutive days.

14. If privileges are occurring only at home, then points in savings can be used to purchase special privileges only when enough points have been earned in school to earn basic privileges.

15. If privileges are occurring in both the school and home settings, then a combination of the above rules applies.

16. When the program is designed for both home and school use, basic privileges are free on weekends.

17. If the program includes both home and school, the purchase of special privileges on weekends is allowed only if the student has earned basic privileges for every day of the school week.

18. Every two weeks, all points are totaled and a new basic privilege average is established. The goal is to challenge the student to improve and work toward more adaptive behavior.

SELP CASE ILLUSTRATION: MICHAEL

Michael, age nine, had been having severe difficulties in school for at least a year. Although he was on grade level academically, he was having problems following classroom rules, paying attention, completing class work, turning in his homework, and getting along with other children. Most recently, Michael was showing evidence of "fresh talk" as well as excessive teasing of other children. His failures were considered serious enough to warrant numerous discussions between his parents, Mr. and Mrs. Jones, and his various teachers. Michael's present teacher, Ms. Smith, was very concerned because she noted that Michael seemed more "sad." She found that she often had to repeat herself over and over to get him to listen. When this failed, she resorted to reprimands, warnings, detentions, and parent conferences. Nothing seemed to work.

The school psychologist conducted interviews with Mr. and Mrs. Jones, Michael, and his teacher. Psychological testing and a learning evaluation were used to gather more information. A sharing conference with all parties resulted in a treatment plan that would begin with the implementation of SELP.

First, a five-day baseline was taken without Michael's knowledge to determine his level of performance on each of the four target behaviors. Baseline performance was recorded on the daily scorecard. Michael had some very good days and some very bad days, with points earned per day ranging from a high of 65 to a low of 10, with an average of 28 points per day. As a result, Michael needed to earn 31 points per day (i.e., 10 percent of 28 =2.8, added to 28 equals 30.8) to earn his basic privileges.

Mr. and Mrs. Jones consulted a list of reinforcers, like the ones in Appendix A, to develop basic privileges and special privileges for Michael. Once they recorded these privileges on the SELP Reward Menu they were ready to explain the program to Michael. Prepared for a less than enthusiastic response, they were surprised that Michael was eager to have the opportunity to gain special privileges and looked forward to the start of the program.

SELP began, and for the first few days Michael did quite well, earning all his basic privileges. However, Mr. and Mrs. Jones were wise enough to know that this was the "honeymoon period." Sure enough, Michael had a terrible day, gained no privileges, had a major temper tantrum, tore up all the recording forms, and actually ran away from home for a few hours. When he finally returned, his parents calmly told him he needed to tape the forms together and that they were going to continue to follow the program.

Every week, Michael's parents compiled the scores from the Daily Scorecard on the Weekly Record Form to record Michael's progress. Every two weeks, they averaged the number of points Michael had earned and revised the points required for him to purchase basic privileges by adding ten to that average.

Over the next few months, Michael began to show steady improvement. Occasionally, setbacks would occur, but they were less frequent, less intense, and of shorter duration. Michael was gradually weaned from the program by entering a phase of self-monitoring whereby he rated his own behavior and checked his ratings against those of his parents.

Mr. and Mrs. Jones continued to use the program independent of formal therapy for the remainder of the school year and discontinued its use over the summer when Michael was away at camp. At the start of the new school year, both parents noted significant improvements in Michael's overall behavior and did not feel a need to reinstate SELP.

Sample SELP Daily Scorecard

Child's name ___Michael_____ Date ___April 17_____

Please rate this student in each category listed below, based on performance during your class period/subject.

10 = excellent

5 = fair

0 = poor

X = not applicable

Class Period/Subject

Category	1	2	3	4	5	6	7	8	9	10	Total
Follows class rules	5	0	5	0	0						10
Completes class work/participates	5	0	5	5	0						15
Completes homework	5	0	0	0	0						5
Gets along with other students	5	0	5	0	0						10
Teacher's initials	MJ	MJ	MJ	MJ	MJ						
Total	20	0	15	5	0						40

Comments: ___Michael seemed to have a rough day today. We talked about how to turn his performance around for tomorrow and he seemed eager to bring up his scores.___

Sample SELP Reward Menu

Child's name ___Michael_____ Date ___April 17_____

Basic Privileges **Points Required**

1. use of computer
2. use of telephone
3. going outside
4. having a friend over

} 31

Basic privileges must be purchased every day.

Special Privileges **Points Required**

1.	extended 30-minute bedtime	5
2.	snack treat	5
3.	use of bike	10
4.	extended 1-hour bedtime (weekends)	10
5.	chore pass	10
6.	choosing dinner menu	10
7.	renting a DVD	15
8.	one friend sleeps over	15
9.	using power tools (with supervision)	25
10.	amusement park	50
11.	10-dollar gift certificate	50
12.	two friends sleep over	100

Note: Special privileges in school can only be purchased if all basic privileges have been earned for two consecutive days.

Sample SELP Weekly Record Form

Child's name ___Michael_____ Week beginning ___May 6_____

Points required for basic privileges _____31_____

Points carried over from previous week _____25_____

	Points Earned	Points Spent	Savings
Monday	40	31	34
Tuesday	35	31	38
Wednesday	50	31	57
Thursday	35	31	61
Friday	25	X	61
Saturday	Basic privileges are free.	X	61
Sunday	Basic privileges are free.	X	61

1. Follows class rules

10 = all rules followed for the entire period

5 = most of the rules followed for the entire period (e.g., runs to get in line)

0 = breaks at least one major rule (e.g., pushes another person)

2. Completes class work or participates in class (whichever is appropriate)

10 = completes 80 to 100% of class work/good participation

5 = completes 60 to 79% of class work/average participation

0 = completes less than 60% of class work/poor participation

3. Completes homework

10 = completes 80 to 100% of homework

5 = completes 60 to 79% of homework

0 = completes less than 60% of homework

4. Gets along with other students

10 = gets along with every student

5 = gets along with most students

0 = one or more major incidents with another student

From *The Behavior Problems Resource Kit,* © 2010 by Michael J. Asher, Steven B. Gordon, Michael C. Selbst, and Mark Cooperberg, Champaign, IL: Research Press (800-519-2707, www.researchpress.com)

SELP Daily Scorecard

Child's name _____ Date _____

Please rate this student in each category listed below, based on performance during your class period/subject.

10 = excellent

5 = fair

0 = poor

X = not applicable

Class Period/Subject

Category	1	2	3	4	5	6	7	8	9	10	Total
Follows class rules	☐	☐	☐	☐	☐	☐	☐	☐	☐	☐	___
Completes class work/participates	☐	☐	☐	☐	☐	☐	☐	☐	☐	☐	___
Completes homework	☐	☐	☐	☐	☐	☐	☐	☐	☐	☐	___
Gets along with otherstudents	☐	☐	☐	☐	☐	☐	☐	☐	☐	☐	___
Teacher's initials	___	___	___	___	___	___	___	___	___	___	
Total	☐	☐	☐	☐	☐	☐	☐	☐	☐	☐	___

Comments: _____

_____

_____

_____

From *The Behavior Problems Resource Kit,* © 2010 by Michael J. Asher, Steven B. Gordon, Michael C. Selbst, and Mark Cooperberg, Champaign, IL: Research Press (800-519-2707, www.researchpress.com)

SELP Reward Menu

Child's name _____ Date _____

Basic Privileges   **Points Required**

1. _____ ⎫
2. _____ ⎬ _____
3. _____ ⎪
4. _____ ⎭

Basic privileges must be purchased every day.

Special Privileges   **Points Required**

1. _____   _____
2. _____   _____
3. _____   _____
4. _____   _____
5. _____   _____
6. _____   _____
7. _____   _____
8. _____   _____
9. _____   _____
10. _____   _____
11. _____   _____
12. _____   _____

Note: Special privileges in school can only be purchased if all basic privileges have been earned for two consecutive days.

From *The Behavior Problems Resource Kit,* © 2010 by Michael J. Asher, Steven B. Gordon, Michael C. Selbst, and Mark Cooperberg, Champaign, IL: Research Press (800-519-2707, www.researchpress.com)

SELP Weekly Record Form

Child's name _____ Week beginning _____

Points required for basic privileges _____

Points carried over from previous week _____

	Points Earned	**Points Spent**	**Savings**
Monday	_____	_____	_____
Tuesday	_____	_____	_____
Wednesday	_____	_____	_____
Thursday	_____	_____	_____
Friday	_____	_____	_____
Saturday	Basic privileges are free.	_____	_____
Sunday	Basic privileges are free.	_____	_____

Home Environment Learning Program (HELP)

The Home Environment Learning Program (HELP) assists parents and mental health professionals in establishing more positive home behaviors. HELP provides a means to set a baseline and monitor the behaviors required of children and adolescents at home. Like the School Environment Learning Program (SELP), it is a point system.

The program is implemented in the home setting by parents of children and adolescents described as lacking in self-control. These children, ranging from preschool age through adolescence, are often diagnosed by mental health professionals as having oppositional defiant disorder, conduct disorder, or autism spectrum disorder. Within a school setting, these children may or may not be classified. The HELP program has also been used successfully with children within the normal range of development who may not reach criterion for a formal diagnosis.

HELP requires an active commitment on the part of parents who carry out the program, in consultation with a therapist. The program may seem complicated initially, but it is easily understood once put into effect, and significant success is likely. However, the program needs to be conducted as written to ensure its integrity, as modifications may decrease effectiveness. The work is well worth it in terms of improved parent-child relationships.

The rest of this discussion describes program procedures and the use of all necessary forms:

- HELP Behavior Rating Scale
- HELP Reward Menu
- HELP Weekly Record Form

Samples of the last two forms are included for a case illustration. Reproducible forms are at the end of this section.

SUMMARY OF HELP RULES

1. Each day of the week is divided into three time periods: morning, afternoon, and evening.

   On school days, *morning* refers to the time from waking to departure for school, *afternoon* refers to departure from school through return home and dinner, and *evening* refers to the time after dinner through bedtime.

   On weekends and holidays, *morning* refers to waking through lunch (or noon), *afternoon* refers to the period after lunch through dinner, and *evening* refers to the period after dinner through bedtime.

2. The parent rates the child's behavior during each time period, using the HELP Behavior Rating Scale. The scale given here is suggested as a guideline; it may be modified to describe the behavior of the individual child more accurately.

3. The rating scale is further defined for each child by specifying observable actions that would constitute each score. For example, a score of 25 for the morning period on a school day might be defined as follows:

   • gets out of bed by 7:00 A.M.

   • dresses and washes self by 7:30 A.M. with no reminders

   • talks pleasantly to all family members

   • puts breakfast dishes in sink with no reminders

   • gets to school by bus

   This type of description is developed for each time period during the day.

4. The scoring is done for seven days privately, without informing the child, in order to establish a pretreatment baseline or "behavioral X-ray."

5. Parents establish basic privileges, which consist of approximately four activities that are meaningful to the child and that can be controlled by the parents (e.g., use of computer for the day, going outside, bedtime, special snacks, etc.).

6. The child must earn a predetermined number of points in order to obtain basic privileges the next day. The number of points required is the child's baseline average plus 10 percent. For example, if after a seven-day period of private record keeping, a child earns an average of 30 points per day, then the number of points required for basic privileges would be 33 points per day (30 + 3 = 33).

7. At the end of each time period, the parent records the total number of points earned and informs the child of the rating. At the end of the day, the parent informs the child whether or not basic privileges have been earned for the next day.

8. All points earned must be used for basic privileges whether the child wants them or not. This means a child cannot forego spending points for basic privileges in order to deposit them into savings and thereby use them later to purchase special privileges.

9. If the child earns more points in a day than are needed for basic privileges, then the extra points are deposited into savings and can be used to purchase special privileges.

10. Special privileges are arranged in advance and posted on the HELP Reward Menu (e.g., fishing = 50 points, sleepover = 75 points, etc.).

11. If the child fails to earn the points needed for basic privileges, then the points earned that day are automatically lost. This does not apply to points already in savings.

12. Points in savings can be spent on special privileges only after one day of earning basic privileges.

13. Every two weeks, points are totaled and a new basic privilege average is established. The goal is to challenge the child to improve and work toward more adaptive behavior.

HELP CASE ILLUSTRATION: TANYA

Tanya, age nine, was referred by Mr. and Mrs. Phillips' pediatrician after lengthy discussions among her parents, teacher, and guidance counselor. Although Tanya was on grade level in school, she was having increasing difficulty following classroom rules, paying attention, and getting along with other children. Her problems were not considered serious enough to warrant a referral to the school's child study team. However, Mr. and Mrs. Phillips were very concerned because Tanya was very difficult to manage at home. They often had to repeat themselves over and over again to get her to listen. When this failed, they resorted to screaming, threatening, and, on occasion, spanking. Nothing seemed to work. In addition, Tanya was beginning to show evidence of "fresh talk" as well as excessive teasing directed toward her younger sister. Mr. and Mrs. Phillips were at their wit's end, and their own relationship was starting to show the strain.

Interviews were held with Mr. and Mrs. Phillips, Tanya, and her teacher. Psychological testing and a learning evaluation were used to gather more information. A sharing conference with all parties resulted in a treatment plan that would begin with the implementation of behavioral parent training and the use of HELP.

First, the rating scale for Tanya was refined and a seven-day baseline was conducted. Baseline performance showed that Tanya had some very good days and some very bad days. Her scores each day ranged from a high of 65 points to a low of 10 points, with an average of 20 points per day. It was decided that Tanya would need 22 points per day (20 + 2 = 22) to earn all her basic privileges.

Mr. and Mrs. Phillips reviewed a list of reinforcers (see Appendix A) to develop basic privileges and special privileges for Tanya. Once her parents recorded these privileges on the HELP Reward Menu, they were ready to explain the program to Tanya. Tanya was curious about the program and looked forward to the opportunity to gain special privileges.

As the HELP Weekly Record Form shows, Tanya did well for the first week, earning all her basic privileges. However, Mr. and Mrs. Phillips suspected that this was the "honeymoon period." Sure enough, Tanya had a terrible day, gained no privileges, had a major temper tantrum, tore up all the recording forms, and ran away from home for a few hours. When she finally returned, her parents calmly told her to tape the forms together and that they were going to continue to follow the program.

Every two weeks, Tanya's parents totaled and averaged the points from the HELP Weekly Record Form, then revised the points required for her to purchase basic privileges by adding 10 percent to that average.

Over the next few months, Tanya showed steady improvement. Occasionally, setbacks occurred, but they were less frequent, less intense, and of shorter duration. Tanya was gradually weaned from the program by entering a phase of self-monitoring where she rated her own behavior and checked her ratings against those of her parents.

Mr. and Mrs. Phillips continued to use the program independent of formal therapy for the remainder of the school year but discontinued its use over the summer. At the start of the new school year, both parents noted significant improvements in Tanya's overall behavior and did not feel a need to reinstate HELP.

Sample HELP Reward Menu

Child's name <u>Tanya</u>   Date <u>January 12</u>

Basic Privileges   **Points Required**

1. <u>use of TV</u>
2. <u>use of computer</u>   }   <u>22</u>
3. <u>use of telephone</u>
4. <u>going outside to play</u>

Basic privileges must be purchased every day.

Special Privileges   **Points Required**

1.	added 30 minutes of computer time	5
2.	extended 30-minute bedtime	5
3.	use of Mom's nail polish	12
4.	chore pass	12
5.	video game rental	15
6.	DVD rental	15
7.	sleepover at friend's house	22
8.	one friend sleeps over	22
9.	using kitchen to make cookies	25
10.	going to movies	25
11.		
12.		

Note: Special privileges in school can only be purchased if all basic privileges have been earned for two consecutive days.

Sample HELP Weekly Record Form

Child's name ___Tanya_____ Week beginning ___January 12_____

Points required for basic privileges _____22_____

Points carried over from previous week ____none____

		Points Earned	Total	Points Spent	Savings
Monday	morning	+ 25			
	afternoon	+ 15			
	evening	+ 15	+55	22	33
Tuesday	morning	− 25			
	afternoon	+ 15			
	evening	+ 15	+5	0	33
Wednesday	morning	+ 5			
	afternoon	+ 25			
	evening	+ 15	+45	22	56
Thursday	morning	+ 25			
	afternoon	+ 25			
	evening	− 25	+25	50	9
Friday	morning	− 25			
	afternoon	− 25			
	evening	− 15	−65	0	9
Saturday	morning	+ 5			
	afternoon	+ 5			
	evening	+ 15	+25	22	12
Sunday	morning	+ 15			
	afternoon	+ 5			
	evening	+ 25	+45	22	35

Note: On Tuesday and Friday, Tanya earned fewer than 22 points, the number required for basic privileges. Therefore, she lost the points she earned on those days.

Please make any revisions in the space provided after each rating.

25 Points

The child does everything that is asked with a pleasant attitude. No reminders have to be given. The child gets along with all members of the family by talking pleasantly. This also applies to people outside the home. The child listens attentively without interruptions. Instructions are followed with a willing attitude to learn and/or take correction.

_____

_____

15 Points

The child does everything asked with a pleasant attitude but requires an occasional reminder. The child may have one minor disagreement with a family member, but this does not involve name calling or physical aggression. This also applies to people outside the family. Instructions are followed with a slightly less than willing attitude to learn and/or take correction.

_____

_____

5 Points

The child does everything asked but with some arguing. The child may have one minor disagreement with family members, or any disagreement involving name calling. This also applies to people outside the family. There may be several interruptions. Instructions are followed with a slightly less than willing attitude to learn and/or take correction.

_____

_____

0 Points

The child uses name calling , screams, makes threatening gestures or comments, punches or kicks objects, throws objects, locks self in room, attacks another person. The child refuses to allow another person to finish speaking by yelling and/or leaving the room. The child refuses to follow instructions.

_____

_____

From *The Behavior Problems Resource Kit,* © 2010 by Michael J. Asher, Steven B. Gordon, Michael C. Selbst, and Mark Cooperberg, Champaign, IL: Research Press (800-519-2707, www.researchpress.com)

HELP Reward Menu

Child's name _____ Date _____

Basic Privileges   **Points Required**

1. _____ ⎫
2. _____ ⎬ _____
3. _____ ⎭
4. _____

Basic privileges must be purchased every day.

Special Privileges   **Points Required**

1. _____   _____
2. _____   _____
3. _____   _____
4. _____   _____
5. _____   _____
6. _____   _____
7. _____   _____
8. _____   _____
9. _____   _____
10. _____ _____
11. _____ _____
12. _____ _____

Note: Special privileges in school can only be purchased if all basic privileges have been earned for two consecutive days.

From *The Behavior Problems Resource Kit,* © 2010 by Michael J. Asher, Steven B. Gordon, Michael C. Selbst, and Mark Cooperberg, Champaign, IL: Research Press (800-519-2707, www.researchpress.com)

Child's name _____ Week beginning _____

Points required for basic privileges _____

Points carried over from previous week _____

		Points Earned	Total	Points Spent	Savings
Monday	morning	_____		_____	_____
	afternoon	_____		_____	_____
	evening	_____	_____	_____	_____
Tuesday	morning	_____		_____	_____
	afternoon	_____		_____	_____
	evening	_____	_____	_____	_____
Wednesday	morning	_____		_____	_____
	afternoon	_____		_____	_____
	evening	_____	_____	_____	_____
Thursday	morning	_____		_____	_____
	afternoon	_____		_____	_____
	evening	_____	_____	_____	_____
Friday	morning	_____		_____	_____
	afternoon	_____		_____	_____
	evening	_____	_____	_____	_____
Saturday	morning	_____		_____	_____
	afternoon	_____		_____	_____
	evening	_____	_____	_____	_____
Sunday	morning	_____		_____	_____
	afternoon	_____		_____	_____
	evening	_____	_____	_____	_____

APPENDIX A

REINFORCEMENT INVENTORIES AND POSITIVE NOTE HOME

It's important to determine which consequences are salient for a child for positive reinforcement to be effective. The Reinforcement Inventory for Children and the Reinforcement Inventory for Adolescents list common reinforcers for children and adolescents at school and at home.

These inventory forms can be used as part of a structured interview or administered independently. Parents and school personnel can include photographs or picture communication symbols to the text. This visual support increases the child's ability to discriminate among reinforcers and makes the intervention more concrete and child friendly.

From the child's choice of reinforcers on the inventory, the adult can construct a reward menu like the example on the next page.

School personnel can complete the Positive Note Home either on a regular basis or following student's demonstration of a desired behavior. This approach "catches the child being good," a phrase often used to emphasize the importance of identifying and reinforcing behaviors to strengthen. The Positive Note Home contains more than fifteen items so the staff member can efficiently communicate positive feedback to the parents. Additional behaviors may be written on the form, allowing for behavior-specific feedback.

Sample Reward Menu

Reward	Points
Ice cream	24
Trip to McDonald's or Wendy's	40
Movie theater	60
Movie night at home	30
Dunkin' Donuts	20
Pokémon card	6
Game night	12
Trip to playground	15
Bowling	30
Webkinz time on computer 30-minute maximum	8
Half hour of evening educational television	12
Chuck E. Cheese	50
Library visit	8

Reinforcement Inventory for Children

Child's name _____ Date _____

Form completed by _____

Place a checkmark next to all reinforcers that may be effective in this specific situation and for this particular child.

SCHOOL

- ☐ Having extra or longer recess
- ☐ Erasing boards
- ☐ Helping the custodian or another staff member
- ☐ Telephoning parent
- ☐ Being group leader
- ☐ Going to the principal's office on an errand
- ☐ Fixing bulletin board
- ☐ Going to the library or media center
- ☐ Tutoring another student
- ☐ Running errands
- ☐ Getting a "good note" to give to parents
- ☐ Being hall monitor
- ☐ Chewing gum in class
- ☐ Playing a game
- ☐ Getting positive comments on homework

- ☐ Listening to MP3 player or CDs
- ☐ Having picture taken
- ☐ Helping librarian
- ☐ Getting stars or stickers
- ☐ Sharpening pencils
- ☐ Being cafeteria helper
- ☐ Viewing film or DVD
- ☐ Getting a badge to be worn all day
- ☐ Demonstrating a hobby to class
- ☐ Having a party
- ☐ Getting a special certificate
- ☐ Getting a drink of water
- ☐ Being principal's helper
- ☐ Having choice of seat mate
- ☐ Having a snack
- ☐ Watching self on video

- ☐ Getting free activity time (puzzles, games)
- ☐ Playing an instrument
- ☐ Getting a happy face on paper
- ☐ Having story time
- ☐ Participating in crafts activities
- ☐ Having lunch with teacher
- ☐ Being head of the lunch line
- ☐ Making a video
- ☐ Using class computer
- ☐ Other _____

_____

_____

HOME

Social

- ☐ Hugs
- ☐ Pats on the back
- ☐ Kisses
- ☐ High-fives
- ☐ Verbal praise
- ☐ Other _____

   _____

   _____

Privileges or Activities

- ☐ Dressing up in adult clothing
- ☐ Opening coffee can
- ☐ Taking a trip to the park
- ☐ Helping make dessert
- ☐ Playing with friends
- ☐ Feeding the baby
- ☐ Reading a bedtime story
- ☐ Having later bedtime
- ☐ Playing on swing set
- ☐ Going to movies
- ☐ Spending a night with friends or grandparents
- ☐ Using stereo

- ☐ Riding next to the window in the car
- ☐ Going to a ball game
- ☐ Making a home video
- ☐ Eating out
- ☐ Choosing menu for meal
- ☐ Using tools
- ☐ Going someplace alone
- ☐ Going someplace with a parent
- ☐ Making a phone call
- ☐ Baking something
- ☐ Gardening
- ☐ Planning a day's activities
- ☐ Riding bicycle
- ☐ Choosing television program
- ☐ Skipping chores
- ☐ Going on a fishing trip
- ☐ Camping in backyard
- ☐ Watching DVD in car
- ☐ Other _____

   _____

   _____

Material

- ☐ Toys
- ☐ Snacks
- ☐ Pets
- ☐ Own bedroom
- ☐ Books
- ☐ Clothing
- ☐ Other _____

   _____

   _____

Token

- ☐ Money
- ☐ Allowance
- ☐ Stars on chart
- ☐ Own bank account
- ☐ Other _____

   _____

   _____

Reinforcement Inventory for Children (page 2 of 2)

Reinforcement Inventory for Adolescents

Child's name _____ Date _____

Form completed by _____

Place a checkmark next to all reinforcers that may be effective in this specific situation and for this particular adolescent.

SCHOOL

- ☐ Being group leader
- ☐ Running errands
- ☐ Playing games
- ☐ Watching films or DVDs
- ☐ Playing an instrument
- ☐ Making a video
- ☐ Chewing gum in class
- ☐ Having free activity time
- ☐ Having an extended lunch period
- ☐ Participating in school trips

- ☐ Having the opportunity to improve grades
- ☐ Wearing a baseball cap in class
- ☐ Being in charge of class discussion
- ☐ Serving as hall monitor
- ☐ Listening to MP3 or CD
- ☐ Having a homework pass
- ☐ Tutoring another student
- ☐ Demonstrating a hobby to the class

- ☐ Developing a school radio show
- ☐ Playing a video game
- ☐ Being on sports team
- ☐ Being dismissed early from class
- ☐ Other _____
  _____
  _____

HOME

Social

- ☐ Smiles
- ☐ Hugs
- ☐ Attention when talking
- ☐ Being asked for opinion
- ☐ Winks
- ☐ Verbal praise
- ☐ Head nods

- ☐ Thumbs-up sign
- ☐ Other _____
  _____
  _____

Privileges or Activities

- ☐ Dating privileges
- ☐ Car privileges

- ☐ Getting driver's license
- ☐ Reading
- ☐ Having extended curfew
- ☐ Staying up late
- ☐ Staying overnight with friends
- ☐ Having time off from chores

From *The Behavior Problems Resource Kit,* © 2010 by Michael J. Asher, Steven B. Gordon, Michael C. Selbst, and Mark Cooperberg, Champaign, IL: Research Press (800-519-2707, www.researchpress.com)

- ☐ Having an opportunity to earn money
- ☐ Selecting television program
- ☐ Using family camera
- ☐ Participating in activities with friends
- ☐ Having a part-time job
- ☐ Having friends over
- ☐ Taking dance or music lessons
- ☐ Redecorating room
- ☐ Skating
- ☐ Listening to stereo
- ☐ Having additional time on telephone
- ☐ Choosing own bedtime
- ☐ Taking trip alone on bus or airplane
- ☐ Other _____
  _____
  _____

Material

- ☐ Favorite meal
- ☐ Clothes
- ☐ Books
- ☐ Bicycle
- ☐ Electric razor
- ☐ Own room
- ☐ Own television
- ☐ Watch
- ☐ Make-up
- ☐ MP3 or CDs
- ☐ Cell phone
- ☐ Jewelry
- ☐ Computer in room
- ☐ Musical instrument
- ☐ Other _____
  _____
  _____

Token

- ☐ Extra money
- ☐ Own checking account
- ☐ Allowance
- ☐ Gift certificate
- ☐ Other _____
  _____
  _____

Reinforcement Inventory for Adolescents (page 2 of 2)

Positive Note Home

Your child, _____, has received this note home as a result of positive

behavior today at _____ School. Your child's behavior exemplifies the

type of behavior that we aspire to in our school. Congratulations!

Your child exhibited strong behavior:

☐ following directions   ☐ helping the teacher

☐ helping another student   ☐ great homework

☐ outstanding participation   ☐ excellent test or quiz

☐ working cooperatively   ☐ working independently

☐ managing anger   ☐ taking responsibility

☐ problem solving   ☐ communicating effectively

☐ improving grades   ☐ improving homework

☐ strong creativity   ☐ improving organization

☐ other _____

Comments: _____

_____

_____

_____   _____

Teacher's name   Date

From *The Behavior Problems Resource Kit,* © 2010 by Michael J. Asher, Steven B. Gordon, Michael C. Selbst, and Mark Cooperberg, Champaign, IL: Research Press (800-519-2707, www.researchpress.com)

APPENDIX B

SAMPLE BEHAVIOR AND SOCIAL SKILLS INTERVENTION PLANS

Case Example: Billy

Case Example: Samantha

CASE EXAMPLE: BILLY

Billy is a five-year-old male preschooler diagnosed with an autism spectrum disorder. He presents with global developmental delays, including cognitive deficits, limited expressive language skills (i.e., he speaks in up to three-word phrases when prompted), motor delays, significant difficulties with social skills and age-appropriate play, delays in daily living skills, and preacademic delays. Billy displays various challenging behaviors that interfere with his ability to benefit from educational programming. His parents have significant difficulty managing his behavior at home and in the community. Problem behaviors include at least the following: physical aggression toward other children and adults, self-injurious behavior on occasion, poor compliance with adult requests, tantrums including dropping to the floor and crying, and trouble remaining seated. He is in a new school, and his behaviors have increased in frequency.

Sample Behavior Intervention Plan for Billy

Please use additional pages if necessary.

Child's name   Billy   Date   October 10

Age   5   Grade   Preschool

Form completed by   Dr. Coop

1. **Describe the target behavior (the behavior to be reduced) in sufficient detail so two independent observers could understand it.**

   Billy demonstrates tantrum behavior, which includes a combination of behaviors: physical aggression toward other children and adults (defined as hitting or attempting to hit others with his open hand or closed fist, kicking or attempting to kick by striking his leg against the body of another individual), self-injurious behavior (defined as hitting himself with an open hand or closed fist, scratching his arms or legs by digging his nails into his skin, or pinching his skin), and dropping to the floor (which may be accompanied by crying).

2. **Describe baseline results, or the current level of behavior, including dates data were collected, frequency, duration, range of frequency, and/or intensity.**

   Baseline data were collected for 10 days during the end of September. Billy displayed the target behaviors an average of 2.3 times per day. The duration of the target behaviors averaged 9.5 minutes per episode. The behavior began on the first school day in early September. Prior history indicates that this behavior occurred with less frequency at his previous school.

3. **List circumstances under which the target behavior occurs or does not occur.**

   Billy is much more compliant when he is engaged in preferred activities, such as gross motor movement, outdoor play, and lunch. The target behavior is more likely to occur when he leaves these activities to return to the classroom, when demands are made in the classroom, and when staff members are in close proximity to him.

4. **List prior interventions (if any) and the effectiveness of these interventions.**

Staff have used a goldfish cracker or a sticker when Billy complies with a demand. Staff have physically prompted Billy to sit and transition, but this rarely is effective. Billy had access to an augmentative communication system at home beginning in August. In August, the speech/language pathologist at his new school assessed Billy's understanding of the augmentative communication system and has been teaching him to communicate his wants and needs via this system. This has been helpful. When Billy hits, staff members verbally reprimand Billy by saying, "No hitting," but the hitting continues.

5. **Place a checkmark next to and explain probable function(s) of the behavior. All functions of behavior should be understood as the child's attempt to communicate his or her needs.**

☑ Escape and/or avoid task

Billy tends to display the target behavior to avoid transitioning or engaging in tasks. He is much more compliant during physical education, lunch, and outside play. Small-group and one-on-one work sessions result in more frequent occurrence of the target behavior.

☐ Escape and/or avoid social situation

☑ Adult attention

The behavior increases when staff members are working with another student. When staff members are providing him with reinforcement or engaging him in a preferred activity, he relates positively with the staff member.

☐ Peer attention

☐ Tangible object

☑ Tangible activity

Billy prefers gross motor activities in the gym and times he can play sports and run around outside. He does not particularly enjoy hands-on classroom activities, such as puzzles, Legos, or blocks.

☑ Automatic positive reinforcement (seeks to initiate or continue pleasurable sensory stimulation)

Billy prefers movement activities, including jumping, kicking a ball, swinging, and throwing a ball. He does not like to sit in a traditional classroom seat but will sit on the bench during lunch. He does hit, scratch, and pinch himself when he is calm but is much more likely to display these self-injurious behaviors when upset.

☐ Automatic negative reinforcement (seeks to reduce or eliminate uncomfortable sensory stimulation)

Sample Behavior Intervention Plan for Billy (page 2 of 6)

6. **Identify and list "replacement behaviors" to be developed and reinforced to replace negative/target behaviors. (Replacement behaviors are the prosocial or appropriate behaviors that will help the child communicate wants or needs.)**

   a. Billy will communicate his wants and needs via his augmentative communication device, sign language, gesture, and/or word approximation. Needs and wants include (1) to get staff attention, (2) to gain access to preferred activities, (3) to request a break from tasks/demands, and (4) to seek automatic positive reinforcement.

   b. When told to sit or shown a picture of sitting at his desk, Billy will walk over to his desk and sit without the physical assistance of staff.

   c. Billy will remain seated at his desk during individual and small-group time for at least five minutes of an activity or until task completion (whichever is less).

   d. Billy will appropriately transition between activities throughout the day without displaying the target behavior.

   e. Billy will choose a reward from a field of two prior to each activity or task demand.

7. **Describe positive supports/ interventions to develop or strengthen replacement behaviors.**

   a. Functional communication training will be offered to improve communication skills, including direct teaching by and consultation from the speech/language pathologist, with carryover strategies implemented by staff and parents.

   b. A picture of the upcoming activity will be provided prior to every transition.

   c. Reinforcement will be offered (choice of two reinforcers) at the same time the request is made. Picture representation of reward will be used, together with verbal request (e.g., "Work, then . . ."). A reinforcement inventory will be completed first by staff and parents to determine highly preferred rewards. Reinforcement will be given when Billy completes an activity or when he sits for a period of five minutes during group activity. If he hits during the activity, he will be told "No hitting. Quiet hands." The timer will be restarted, and no reinforcer will be given.

   d. Task choice will be used throughout the day, including two choices for where Billy can sit, what writing instrument he can use, what task he wants, etc.

   e. Billy will be provided with noncontingent opportunities throughout the day (at least every 15 minutes) to manipulate clay or squeeze a rubber ball to assist in reducing his need to scratch, pinch, and hit himself or others.

8. **Identify the reinforcement schedule (e.g., fixed or variable interval or fixed or variable ratio schedule).**

Billy will be reinforced upon completion of a task during one-on-one work or after sitting for five minutes during group activities without displaying the target behavior. Behavior-specific praise ("Good working," "Nice sitting") will be provided throughout the activity and will be paired with the tangible reward.

9. **Specify the procedures to implement when the target behavior occurs (e.g., planned ignoring, Sit and Think, verbal or physical prompt, correction procedure).**

   a. When Billy displays the target behavior, staff will provide one prompt to encourage him, reminding him of the reward he may earn. If he displays the behavior again, a second prompt will be given. If he displays the target behavior again, staff will withdraw all attention from Billy. This will continue for 10 minutes, after which staff will state the request again, telling and showing him that he can earn the reward he chose. If noncompliance continues, then a prompt should be given again 10 minutes later and again 10 minutes later. Reinforcement choices should not be provided at school/home unless Billy complies with the request.

   b. If Billy attempts to aggress toward staff or peers, he will be told, "No hitting. Quiet hands." The timer will be restarted, and no reward will be given. If he aggresses a second time, then the same redirection will be given. If he aggresses a third time, staff should withdraw attention immediately.

   c. Staff should attempt to block Billy's aggressive behavior, ensuring safety of all individuals. If the aggressive behavior escalates at any time or does not diminish after a period of 10 minutes, then Billy should be escorted to a calm area ("safe haven") in which he will be properly supervised. Once he is calm, staff members should introduce a series of brief, mastered tasks for a period of five minutes, providing behavior-specific praise.

   d. Once staff members have determined that he is calm, Billy should be escorted back to the classroom. If there is any physical contact between Billy and staff members and/or students, the individuals involved should be seen by the school nurse.

10. **List materials required (e.g., timer, counter, data sheets, token board, picture symbols).**

Individual picture schedule, picture reward board, augmentative communication device, clay/squeeze ball, timer, home-school communication book, reinforcement inventory

11. **List the environmental changes/classroom modifications (e.g., preferential seating, lighting, calm area, sound amplification, type of desk/chair).**

The classroom and materials should be arranged so that there are always two choices where Billy can sit and two choices for materials (e.g., two different pencils, crayons, puzzles, etc.).

12. **Describe data collection and management system (e.g., event recording, duration recording, time sampling, interval recording, permanent product, intensity rating, anecdotal recording).**

The School ABC Recording Form (p. 53) will be used to maintain daily data regarding date, time, location, antecedent (e.g., demand/activity), behavior (e.g., compliant, noncompliant), and consequences following target behavior. Data will be graphed on a weekly basis.

13. **Describe conditions under which the supports/interventions will be implemented.**

These procedures will be implemented on a daily basis across environments, with the program being monitored by the teacher, behavioral consultant, and case manager.

14. **Describe conditions under which the supports/interventions will be terminated.**

The plan will continue to be implemented until the target behavior occurs an average of one or fewer times daily over a 10-day period. Then the plan will be modified so that a longer period of on-task behavior, with greater task completion, is required prior to providing the reward. It is anticipated that the target behavior may initially worsen during the first month. If the behavior continues to worsen beyond a four-week period or if the safety of staff, peers, or Billy becomes a significant issue at any time, the team will schedule a meeting within 24 hours to discuss the plan.

15. **Describe the plan for parent involvement (e.g., sharing data summary, generalization strategies, parent data collection or reinforcement, information exchange between school and home).**

a. Copies of the School ABC Recording Form will be provided to the parents on a weekly basis. Information regarding Billy's progress will be provided daily via a home-school communication book.

b. Consultation will be provided to the parents via meetings every other month with the teacher, behavioral consultant, and case manager to ensure consistent programming at home, to discuss Billy's progress, and to answer any questions.

c. Parents will maintain regular appointments with Billy's private psychiatrist and will provide the school with any medication changes or other recommendations from the psychiatrist.

16. **Provide the frequency of review.**

Once a week review of the data; monthly meetings with case manager; every other month meeting with the entire team, including parents and behavioral consultant.

17. **Is informed consent required?**   ☑ Yes   ☐ No

Date of implementation ___October 10___   Baseline rate _2.3 times/day, 9.5 mins. avg. duration_

Date of review ___December 10___   Baseline rate ___—___

Date of termination ___—___   Baseline rate ___—___

Sample Behavior Intervention Plan for Billy (page 6 of 6)

Sample Social Skills Intervention Plan for Billy

Please use additional pages if necessary.

Child's name ___Billy_____ Date ___October 10_____

Age ___5_____ Grade _____Preschool_____

Form completed by _____Dr. Coop_____

1. Identify the specific deficit in social behavior.

a. What is the means of assessment (e.g., social skills rating scale, observation, etc.)?

Billy was observed in his classroom by Dr. Coop on September 21, between 11:00 a.m. until 12:30 p.m. Dr. Coop spoke with Billy's teacher, Mrs. Johnson, following the observation. Mrs. Johnson and Billy's parents completed the teacher and parent forms of a social skills rating scale.

b. What are the identified deficits in social skills (e.g., conversational skills, empathy, anger management, interpersonal problem solving)?

Billy does not appropriately manage his anger. He does not identify his feelings or express them to others. When he becomes angry, he has tantrums, throwing himself to the floor and crying.

c. What is the estimated frequency of the social skill deficit? (How often is the deficit displayed?)

Mrs. Johnson reported that Billy has tantrums about five times a week, or once a day.

d. Where does the skill deficit occur (e.g., classroom, playground, lunch room, in the community, at home)?

Billy primarily has tantrums in the classroom but has also displayed these tantrums at home and in the community.

e. With whom does the skill deficit occur (e.g., same-aged peers, older children, younger children, adults)?

Billy displays tantrum behaviors most often when he is with adults, but also occasionally when he is with his older brother.

f. What are the antecedents, the circumstances that set the occasion for the skill deficit to occur?

When Billy is directed to stop an activity he finds enjoyable, he is most likely to have a tantrum. He will also have tantrums when his brother takes away a favorite toy.

g. What circumstances rarely set the occasion for the skill deficit to occur?

Billy has never had a tantrum when he is engaged in a preferred activity (playing with blocks, playing on the computer).

h. What are the consequences (circumstances that follow the occurrence of the skill deficit)?

After Billy has a tantrum, Mrs. Johnson speaks with him to help him calm down. In the home setting, his parents do the same, assuring him that he is okay, while also giving him a hug and back rub.

2. **What is the impact of the skill deficit on the following?**

a. school performance

When Billy has his tantrums, he is unable to transition to work time, and he is therefore unable to complete his work. He then has less time to do his work and does not get the same amount of practice and repetition that his peers do.

b. family interactions

When Billy has his tantrums, his brother becomes frustrated and threatens Billy. This harms the nature of their relationship. Billy's tantrums also frustrate his parents, who would like Billy to "roll with the punches" more easily.

c. student's relationship with peers

When Billy has his tantrums, his classmates try to avoid him. This has resulted in several classmates excluding him from invitations to play.

d. student's self-esteem/confidence

Billy complains that he never gets to do what he wants and that others are not fair to him. He has not internalized this problem, so the direct impact on his self-esteem is uncertain.

3. **What are the hypothesized function(s) of the skill deficit? All functions of behavior should be understood as the child's attempt to communicate his or her needs.**

   ☐ Escape and/or avoid task

   ☐ Escape and/or avoid social situation

   ☑ Adult attention

   After Billy engages in tantrum behavior, he receives attention from his teacher and his parents. His peers do not provide attention following such behaviors.

   ☐ Peer attention

   ☑ Tangible object

   Billy most often engages in tantrums when his access to a preferred activity or object is limited by an adult.

   ☑ Tangible activity

   ☐ Automatic positive reinforcement

   ☑ Automatic negative reinforcement

   Billy appears to engage in tantrums when he does not want to clean up his toys.

4. Describe any previous interventions to address social problems and their results.

In the first three weeks of school, Mrs. Johnson has talked to Billy individually when he has a tantrum. This has not reduced the frequency of his tantrums. The same is true in the home setting.

5. Identify the social skill(s) to be taught.

Feelings identification (knowing his feelings) paired with feelings communication (sharing his feelings). Billy will build his "feelings vocabulary" so he can identify and express his emotions using "I feel . . ." statements. He will also be taught how to manage his upset feelings using the Feelings Management Project (pp. 121).

6. Describe the positive behavior supports/interventions to develop or strengthen the identified skill. Describe settings (where?), personnel (who?), examples (what?), and modality (how?).

a. In school, Billy will receive ten minutes of instruction and review with Mrs. Johnson. At home, Billy's parents will spend ten minutes a day providing instruction and review. During the intervention, the adult will review feelings with Billy, using feelings faces charts. The adult will read the feeling while pointing at the face. Billy will state the name of the feeling. The adult will define the feeling and use it in an "I feel . . ." statement. Billy will then provide his own "I feel . . ." statement. After giving his statement, Billy will get to hit the "easy button" or get a high-five.

b. After correctly identifying all feelings on the chart for a week, Billy will progress to the feelings management strategies.

c. After completing that step, Billy will learn each of the coping strategies, one at a time. The 3-D Skills Approach (p. 134) will be used to teach and practice each strategy at home and in school.

Sample Social Skills Intervention Plan for Billy (page 4 of 6)

7. **What interventions will be used when the skill deficit occurs?**

When Billy shows signs of being upset, he will be prompted to identify his feeling. At first, he will be asked to simply name the feeling. When he has mastered this skill, he will then be prompted to provide a complete "I feel . . ." statement. When he identifies his feeling and expresses it, he will then receive behavior-specific praise from the adult as well as a high-five. Billy will then be directed to use one of his coping strategies. The adult will track which strategies Billy chooses and their effectiveness by following the Learning My Feelings Log (p. 123).

8. **Describe the data collection and management system.**

Data will be collected on a daily basis. The School ABC Recording Form (p. 53) will be used to record the antecedent, behavior, and consequence for each tantrum. The identification of feelings, expression of feelings, and use of coping strategies will be listed each day.

9. **List the personnel responsible for each aspect of intervention (i.e., training and practice).**

Mrs. Johnson and Billy's parents will track the above data in school and at home, respectively. Each will practice the intervention on a daily basis.

10. **What is the skill priority list? Please be specific.**

a. Feelings identification—Billy will build his feelings vocabulary.

b. Feeling expression—Billy will express his feelings.

c. Feeling management—Billy will calm down using coping strategies.

11. **What are the conditions (i.e., criteria) under which the next skill will be introduced?**

When Billy has successfully identified each of the feelings on the feelings faces handout for five consecutive days, he will then proceed to the second skill. When he is able to provide feeling statements for each feeling for five consecutive days, he will proceed to feelings management.

12. **Describe the role of parent involvement (e.g., frequency of communication, method of communication, implementation of interventions).**

Billy's parents and Mrs. Johnson will communicate on a daily basis via a communication log book. Billy's parents will practice the intervention on a daily basis.

13. **What is the consultation and review procedure (weekly, bimonthly, monthly, other)?**

Billy's parents and Mrs. Johnson will review the log book on a daily basis. At the end of each week, his performance with each one of the three skills will be totaled and graphed. Mrs. Johnson will discuss progress with child study team personnel. At the end of the first month, the data will be shared with Billy's behavior therapist and Billy's behaviors will continue to be tracked as recommended. Billy's parents and therapist will outline home and community practice. Triggers, settings, and personnel will be identified to help transfer and generalize skills to the community.

Date of implementation ___October 10___   Baseline rate ___1 time/day___

Date of review ___February 17___   Baseline rate ___—___

Date of termination ___—___   Baseline rate ___—___

CASE EXAMPLE: SAMANTHA

Samantha is a 14-year-old female who recently transitioned from middle school to high school. She presents with significant internalizing symptoms, including generalized anxiety and depression. Her symptoms have been evident intermittently during the last several years but have intensified during the last nine months. She experienced much difficulty developing and maintaining friendships at high school. Her grades have declined; she missed more than 15 days of school this year, has arrived to school late many days, and was observed sleeping during the first and last period classes. Samantha stopped participating in all extracurricular activities. She makes up excuses to avoid going out with family members and tends to spend a lot of time in her bedroom.

Sample Behavior Intervention Plan for Samantha

Please use additional pages if necessary.

Child's name ___ Samantha _____ Date _____ November 20 _____

Age _____ 14 _____ Grade ___ 9 _____

Form completed by _____ Ms. Alvarez _____

1. **Describe the target behavior (the behavior to be reduced) in sufficient detail so two independent observers could understand it.**

   Samantha demonstrates symptoms of anxiety and depression, with more significant symptoms during the last nine months. Her grades have declined. She has missed 15 days of school from September to November, has arrived late to school 17 times, and has fallen asleep frequently during her first and last period classes almost daily. She no longer participates in extracurricular activities. Historically, her grades have been Bs and Cs.

2. **Describe baseline results, or the current level of behavior, including dates data were collected, frequency, duration, range of frequency, and/or intensity.**

   Data have been collected from September 1 through November 15 (42 days of school). Samantha has been absent 15 days, late 17 days, and staff members have reported that she falls asleep daily during her first period class (math) and last period class (science). Her participation is slightly better during language arts, during which she has fallen asleep an estimated five times this year. She has only completed two assignments combined for all of her classes. Test and quiz grades have ranged from 0 points to 85, with similar ranges across all subject areas.

3. **List circumstances under which the target behavior occurs or does not occur.**

   Samantha demonstrates fatigue, withdrawal, sleeping, anhedonia, lack of participation, and incomplete work across subject areas. She is more likely to miss first period class due to lateness and sleeping. She will fall asleep during her last period class as well. Samantha tends to be more alert and less depressed during art class. She is a talented artist, per her parents' and teacher's report. Similar symptoms are displayed at home.

4. **List prior interventions (if any) and the effectiveness of these interventions.**

Samantha has been seeing a private therapist inconsistently during the last three years, with the frequency about once a month during the last six months due to difficulty coordinating schedules between the family and therapist. She has met with the school guidance counselor as needed, per Samantha's request. Contact has been three times in the last six months. Incomplete class work has been sent home to be completed. The principal and teacher have met with Samantha's parents twice this year regarding her attendance and mood. A referral was made to see a child psychiatrist, but her parents have not scheduled the appointment yet. Samantha has not been prescribed medication. There has been no observed improvement resulting from these interventions.

5. **Place a checkmark next to and explain probable function(s) of the behavior. All functions of behavior should be understood as the child's attempt to communicate his or her needs.**

☑ Escape and/or avoid task or social situation

Samantha tends to display the target behavior when presented with academic demands, especially when her mood is depressed or anxious. She is more compliant when she is engaged in mastered material and especially artwork and creative tasks.

☑ Escape and/or avoid social situation

Samantha tends to withdraw from peers and adults when she is feeling depressed or anxious. She does not seek out nor accept adult assistance typically, as she prefers to remain alone during these times.

☐ Adult attention

☐ Peer attention

☐ Tangible object

☐ Tangible activity

☐ Automatic positive reinforcement (seeks to initiate or continue pleasurable sensory stimulation)

☐ Automatic negative reinforcement (seeks to reduce or eliminate uncomfortable sensory stimulation)

6. **Identify and list "replacement behaviors" to be developed and reinforced to replace negative/target behaviors. (Replacement behaviors are the prosocial or appropriate behaviors that will help the child communicate wants or needs.)**

   a. Samantha will communicate her emotions with a trusted adult, begin to form positive relationships with adults, and allow adults to assist her as needed.

   b. Samantha will consistently attend counseling sessions with the school's guidance counselor twice a week. She will also consistently attend all appointments with her private therapist and psychiatrist.

   c. Samantha will complete academic tasks at school and home.

   d. Samantha will attend all school days on time and remain awake throughout the day.

7. **Describe positive supports/ interventions to develop or strengthen replacement behaviors.**

   a. Individual counseling will be provided by the guidance counselor twice a week.

   b. Biweekly consultation meetings will be scheduled among the guidance counselor, teachers, principal, special education personnel, and parents.

   c. With consent, consultation between school district personnel and any private professionals working with Samantha.

   d. Modifications to assignments will include opportunities for Samantha to incorporate artwork and creativity. Timelines for assignments can be modified with group agreement.

8. **Identify the reinforcement schedule (e.g., fixed or variable interval or fixed or variable ratio schedule).**

Behavior-specific praise ("Nice job working," "I like the way you arrive to class on time.") will be provided throughout the day.

9. **Specify the procedures to implement when the target behavior occurs (e.g., planned ignoring, Sit and Think, verbal or physical prompt, correction procedure).**

a. Consultation among the school personnel, parents, and private professionals will be ongoing and shall occur immediately following any deterioration in Samantha's mood or behavior.

b. The Happenings-Thoughts-Feeling Reactions Project (p. 127) will be used to help Samantha better understand the link between her thoughts and feelings so she can work at becoming more effective at managing her emotions.

c. Adults should discuss Samantha's feelings and behavior at a time when she is calm, to assist her in processing situations better. The HOTSAP problem-solving approach (p. 129) will be used to help her better choose adaptive solutions and reactions to her problems.

10. **List materials required (e.g., timer, counter, data sheets, token board, picture symbols).**

Behavior-emotion data sheets are needed to assist Samantha to assess her thoughts, feelings, and behavior related to situations.

11. **List the environmental changes/classroom modifications (e.g., preferential seating, lighting, calm area, sound amplification, type of desk/chair).**

The classroom and materials should be arranged so that Samantha can easily see the board and teacher, with few materials on her desk. Distractions should be limited whenever possible. She should be seated near the front of the classroom with positive peer models beside her.

12. **Describe data collection and management system (e.g., event recording, duration recording, time sampling, interval recording, permanent product, intensity rating, anecdotal recording).**

Data will be recorded regarding Samantha's attendance, arrival time, frequency and duration of sleeping in class, work completion, and academic performance. Her mood will also be assessed with a depression inventory.

13. **Describe conditions under which the supports/interventions will be implemented.**

These procedures will be implemented on a daily basis across environments, with the program being monitored by the teacher, therapists, behavioral consultant, and case manager.

14. **Describe conditions under which the supports/interventions will be terminated.**

The plan will continue to be implemented throughout the school year, with modifications being made following team consultation meetings.

15. **Describe the plan for parent involvement (e.g., sharing data summary, generalization strategies, parent data collection or reinforcement, information exchange between school and home).**

Samantha's parents plan to maintain regular appointments with her private therapist and will consult with a child psychiatrist. They have agreed to provide information regarding her progress with the appropriate consent forms signed.

16. **Provide the frequency of review.**

Biweekly meetings among school personnel and parents will be scheduled. The frequency of these meetings will be reduced as appropriate.

17. **Is informed consent required?** ☑ Yes ☐ No

Date of implementation ____November 20____ Baseline rate ____15 absences/17 tardies____

Date of review ____April 17____ Baseline rate ____—____

Date of termination ____—____ Baseline rate ____—____

Sample Behavior Intervention Plan for Samantha (page 6 of 6)

Sample Social Skills Intervention Plan for Samantha

Please use additional pages if necessary.

Child's name ___Samantha___ Date ___November 20___

Age ___14___ Grade ___9___

Form completed by ___Ms. Alvarez___

1. Identify the specific deficit in social behavior.

a. What is the means of assessment (e.g., social skills rating scale, observation, etc.)?

Observation, teacher report via interviews and social skills rating scale, parent report via interview and social skills rating scale.

b. What are the identified deficits in social skills (e.g., conversational skills, empathy, anger management, interpersonal problem solving)?

Samantha demonstrates asocial behavior, which includes avoiding social contact with her peers and family members. She avoids starting conversations, phoning/e-mailing/texting her peers, and socializing outside of school, and has terminated participation in extracurricular activities.

c. What is the estimated frequency of the social skill deficit? (How often is the deficit displayed?)

Samantha demonstrates asocial behavior on a daily basis.

d. Where does the skill deficit occur (e.g., classroom, playground, lunch room, in the community, at home)?

Samantha demonstrates asocial behavior in the classroom, lunchroom, in the community, and at home.

e. With whom does the skill deficit occur (e.g., same-aged peers, older children, younger children, adults)?

Samantha demonstrates asocial behavior with her same-aged peers but has fewer difficulties with adults.

f. What are the antecedents, the circumstances that set the occasion for the skill deficit to occur?

Samantha demonstrates asocial behavior with her same-aged peers when there is unstructured time during class, during small-group or partner activities, and during free time at school.

g. What circumstances rarely set the occasion for the skill deficit to occur?

Samantha does not demonstrate asocial behavior during independent work, as she is not required to interact with her peers.

h. What are the consequences (circumstances that follow the occurrence of the skill deficit)?

When Samantha does not interact with her peers, she is often prompted by staff to do so (if it is required for small-group or partner work). When she is asocial during nonwork activities, she is often left alone, allowing her to avoid unpleasant anxiety that she experiences during social interactions.

2. What is the impact of the skill deficit on the following?

a. school performance

When Samantha fails to interact appropriately with her peers, it affects group and partner activities. It also impacts her ability to understand academic content and directions, as she does not assertively ask for assistance. Her grades across subjects have recently dropped.

b. family interactions

Samantha does not interact with her family members unless the interaction is initiated by her parents. She will typically provide one-word answers and not elaborate. Her parents report strained relationships at home.

c. student's relationship with peers

Samantha's asocial behavior has led her to avoid peers in all school-based and extracurricular activities. While she had previously maintained three friendships in middle school, she currently has no friends in school and spends no time with same-aged peers outside of the school setting.

d. student's self-esteem/confidence

Samantha reports low self-esteem and confidence in her ability to socialize with others. She completed the Piers-Harris Children's Self-Concept Scale 2, and her self-report was significantly below average for popularity, happiness, and freedom from anxiety.

3. **What are the hypothesized function(s) of the deficit skill? All functions of behavior should be understood as the child's attempt to communicate his or her needs.**

☐ Escape and/or avoid task

☑ Escape and/or avoid social situation

Samantha avoids socializing because she is attempting to avoid interactions with her peers. When she is not directed to speak with her peers, she chooses not to do so. She is able to answer direct questions asked of her but does not initiate conversations with any peers.

☑ Adult attention

Samantha's asocial behavior does result in attention from adults, including her teachers and parents.

☐ Peer attention

☐ Tangible object

☐ Tangible activity

☐ Automatic positive reinforcement

☑ Automatic negative reinforcement

Samantha avoids initiating conversations and has reported that talking to her peers makes her feel anxious. She admitted that she "trusts no one" at her school and that being forced to do so upsets her. By avoiding social interactions, she avoids the upsetting feeling.

4. **Describe any previous interventions to address social problems and their results.**

Samantha has been seeing a private therapist about once a month during the last six months. She has met with the school guidance counselor, per Samantha's request. Staff members observed Samantha with three friends and did not report concern about Samantha's socializing. When asked to talk about why she no longer speaks with these friends, Samantha indicated that she no longer trusts those "rumor mongers." Samantha refused to meet with or talk about this with the counselor or these former friends. No additional interventions have been implemented.

5. **Identify the social skill(s) to be taught.**

   a. Samantha will communicate her wants and needs (specifically, need for staff attention/assistance and need for peer attention/assistance) via oral communication.

   b. Samantha will initiate conversations with her peers.

   c. Samantha will maintain conversations that were started by her peers by appropriately answering questions.

   d. Samantha will engage in one extracurricular activity of her choosing throughout the school year (the activity may change, but she should be enrolled in one activity during the school year).

6. **Describe the positive behavior supports/interventions to develop or strengthen the identified skill. Describe settings (where?), personnel (who?), examples (what?), and modality (how?).**

   a. Samantha will meet with the school counselor twice a week. The counselor will provide training to improve her communication skills, including direct teaching of how to initiate, maintain, and terminate a conversation. Samantha will also receive assistance appropriately sharing her wants and needs via "I feel . . ." and "I want . . ." statements. The counselor will incorporate HTFR (p. 124) and the Feelings Management Project (p. 121) during sessions to help reduce Samantha's anxiety, and she will review with Samantha extracurricular activities available for students.

   b. The counselor will provide written handouts to Samantha's case manager and parents. These handouts will include the expectations for the skills Samantha is developing, including how to express her wants and needs, as well as how to initiate, maintain, and terminate a conversation.

   c. Each teacher will provide behavior-specific praise ("I like the way you asked a question when you were confused") for all socially desirable behaviors and will do the same for other students to minimize the stigma that Samantha may experience were she the only student to receive such feedback.

Sample Social Skills Intervention Plan for Samantha (page 4 of 6)   **229**

d. Teachers will communicate directly with Samantha's case manager and inform her when Samantha engages in any of the desired skills.

e. The team will discuss selection of a peer buddy with strong interpersonal skills to assist Samantha in developing her communication and trust with female peers. With approval from that student and that student's parents, the school counselor will set up an informal meeting with Samantha and the identified peer. They should meet weekly during school hours.

7. What interventions will be used when the skill deficit occurs?

a. When Samantha is assigned to a small-group activity or is paired with another student and she does not engage in verbal communication with her partner, she should be prompted to communicate.

b. Samantha will be reinforced upon engagement in any of the skills via behavior-specific praise. Tokens will be distributed by her parents on Friday afternoons after receipt of communication from her case manager.

8. Describe the data collection and management system.

Staff will attempt to observe the occurrence of replacement skills (e.g., communicating needs, initiating conversations, maintained peer interaction and participation in extracurricular activities), then share this information with the case manager on a weekly basis. E-mail will be sent to Samantha's parents each Friday to collect the frequency of these events and will be maintained to determine the improvement in Samantha's social interactions. This data will be shared with staff to increase attention/assistance when needed.

9. List the personnel responsible for each aspect of intervention (i.e., training and practice).

Each teacher should note the occurrence of skills and communicate this information to the case manager on a weekly basis. This data will be compiled by the case manager, who will then send a weekly e-mail to Samantha's parents on Friday afternoons.

10. What is the skill priority list? Please be specific.

a. Samantha's communication to staff and peers for attention/assistance

b. Samantha's initiating conversation with others

c. Samantha's attendance at extracurricular activity

d. Samantha's maintaining conversation

11. **What are the conditions (i.e., criteria) under which the next skill will be introduced?**

   a. Each of Samantha's skills will be introduced sequentially. When she is able to share her feelings and wants on a daily basis, she will progress to the next skill. The counselor will then assist Samantha in selecting from the extracurricular activities that are available for students.

   b. Next, the counselor will incorporate HTFR and the Feelings Management Project during sessions to help reduce anxiety that Samantha is experiencing. When Samantha reports her anxiety with socializing has reached an acceptable level, she will progress to the next skill.

   c. The next set of skills will include training to improve Samantha's conversational skills, and when she has mastered these conversational skills (as evidenced by successfully having a conversation with peers, using the steps), assessment of additional needs will occur.

12. **Describe the role of parent involvement (e.g., frequency of communication, method of communication, implementation of interventions).**

   a. Parents are to receive weekly e-mail communication about Samantha's social behaviors from the case manager. Consultation will be provided to the parents via meetings every other month with the school counselor and case manager.

   b. Samantha and her parents will develop a rewards menu. Parents will offer reinforcement to Samantha in the form of behavior-specific praise and a token for each display of a skill. She will earn one token for each verbal communication of her wants and needs to peers/staff, one token for each conversation maintained, two tokens for each conversation initiated, and one token for each day of participation in extracurricular activities.

   c. Parents will maintain regular appointments with Samantha's private psychiatrist and therapist and will inform the school of any medication changes or other recommendations.

13. **What is the consultation and review procedure (weekly, bimonthly, monthly, other)?**

   Samantha's parents are to receive weekly communication from the case manager via e-mail indicating the frequency of skill use exhibited during the week. Parents will meet with the team every other month to discuss Samantha's progress.

Date of implementation _____ November 20 _____ Baseline rate _____ 1 time/daily _____

Date of review _____ January 20 _____ Baseline rate _____ — _____

Date of termination _____ — _____ Baseline rate _____ — _____

Sample Social Skills Intervention Plan for Samantha (page 6 of 6)   **231**

REFERENCES

Asher, M. J., & Gordon, S. B. (1998). *The AD/HD forms book: Identification, measurement and intervention.* Champaign, IL: Research Press.

Bernstein, G. A., Bernat, D. H., Victor, A. M., & Layne, A. E. (2008). School-based interventions for anxious children: 3-, 6-, and 12-month follow-ups. *Journal of the American Academy of Child & Adolescent Psychiatry, 47(9),* 1039–1047.

Barkley, R. A., Edwards, G., Laneri, M., Fletcher, K., & Metevia, L.(2001). The efficacy of problem-solving communication training alone, behavior management training alone, and their combination for parent-adolescent conflict in teenagers with ADHD and ODD. *Journal of Consulting and Clinical Psychology, 69(6),* 926–941.

Goldstein, A. P., & McGinnis, E. (1997). *Skillstreaming the adolescent: New strategies and perspectives for teaching prosocial skills.* Champaign, IL: Research Press.

Gordon, S. B., & Asher, M. J. (1994). *Meeting the ADD challenge: A practical guide for teachers.* Champaign, IL: Research Press.

Hibbs, E. D., & Jensen, P. S. (2005). Psychosocial treatments for child and adolescent disorders: Empirically based strategies for clinical practice (2nd ed.). Washington, DC, American Psychological Association.

Maughan, D. R., Christiansen, E., Jenson, W. R., Olympia, D., & Clark, E. (2005). Behavioral parent training as a treatment for externalizing behaviors and disruptive behavior disorder: A meta-analysis. *School Psychology Review, 34,* 267–286.

Koegl, C. J., Farrington, D. P., Augimeri, L. K., Day, D. M. (2008). Evaluation of a targeted cognitive-behavioral program for children with conduct problems: The SNAPReg. under 12 outreach project—Service intensity, age and gender effects on short- and long-term outcomes. *Clinical Child Psychology and Psychiatry, 13(3),* 419–434.

Segool, N. K., Carlson, J. S. (2008). Efficacy of cognitive-behavioral and pharmacological treatments for children with social anxiety. *Depression and Anxiety, 25(7),* 620–631.

TADS Team. (2007).The Treatment for Adolescents with Depression Study (TADS): Long-term effectiveness and safety outcomes. *Archives of General Psychiatry, 64(10),* 1132–1144.

ABOUT THE AUTHORS

MICHAEL J. ASHER, PH.D., is a clinical psychologist licensed in New Jersey. He has been at Behavior Therapy Associates, P.A., in Somerset, New Jersey, since 1988. Dr. Asher is board certified in cognitive and behavioral psychology by the American Board of Professional Psychology and is an adjunct assistant professor in the Department of Psychiatry, University of Medicine and Dentistry of the New Jersey–Robert Wood Johnson Medical School, where he supervises psychiatric fellows and teaches a course on child cognitive behavior therapy. He is also a field supervisor for the Graduate School of Applied and Professional Psychology at Rutgers University. He trains staff and consults to public and private schools on how to conduct functional behavioral assessments and write behavior intervention plans. Dr. Asher is the coauthor of several journal articles and two books: *Meeting the ADD Challenge: A Practical Guide for Teachers* and *The ADHD Forms Book: Identification, Measurement, and Intervention* (Research Press). Dr. Asher's professional interests include working with children and adolescents with disruptive behaviors, pervasive developmental delays, and anxiety disorders.

STEVEN B. GORDON, PH.D., founder and director of Behavior Therapy Associates, P.A., is a clinical psychologist licensed in New Jersey. Dr. Gordon is also board certified in cognitive and behavioral psychology by the American Board of Professional Psychology and is a diplomate in behavior therapy. Dr. Gordon is on the faculty at the Graduate School of Applied and Professional Psychology, Rutgers University, where he has taught courses on adult and child behavior therapy for over 30 years, and is an adjunct associate professor in the Department of Psychiatry, University of Medicine and Dentistry of the New Jersey–Robert Wood Johnson Medical School. Dr. Gordon has published numerous articles, presented papers at local and national conferences, and served on the editorial boards of professional journals. He coauthored *Meeting the ADD Challenge: A Practical Guide for Teachers, The ADHD Forms Book: Identification, Measurement, and Intervention* (Research Press), and *A Practical Guide to Behavioral Assessment* (Springer). Dr. Gordon's professional interests involve providing assessment and treatment for individuals diagnosed with autism spectrum disorders, AD/HD, and other disruptive behavior disorders associated with childhood and adolescence. He co-founded and is the executive director of the HI-STEP® Summer Program, an intensive six-week day program for children designed to improve their social skills and problem-solving abilities.

MICHAEL C. SELBST, PH.D., is associate director of Behavior Therapy Associates, P.A. He is a licensed psychologist and a certified school psychologist in New Jersey and Pennsylvania. Dr. Selbst co-founded and is the executive director of the HI-STEP® Summer Program, an intensive six-week day program for children to improve their social skills and problem-solving abilities, and is director of the Weekend to Improve Social Effectiveness (W.I.S.E.). He has extensive experience working with preschool children through adults, including individuals who are gifted, have learning disabilities, or have social-emotional and behavioral difficulties, as well as children with developmental delays, including those with autism and Asperger's syndrome. Dr. Selbst consults to numerous public and private schools, assisting parents, teachers, and mental health professionals. He also conducts expert evaluations and functional behavioral assessments, and writes behavior intervention plans and psychoeducational and psychological evaluations. He has given national and international workshops and presentations on the topics mentioned above, as well as on parenting strategies, depression, and suicide prevention.

MARK COOPERBERG, PH.D., is a licensed psychologist in New Jersey. He earned his doctorate in clinical psychology with a specialization in children and adolescents at Case Western Reserve University after completing his predoctoral internship at the University of Medicine and Dentistry–Robert Wood Johnson Medical School. Dr. Cooperberg served as a counselor at a residential treatment center at the University of Chicago and has extensive experience conducting therapy and evaluations with children, adolescents, adults, and families, including individuals with a wide range of presenting problems. Dr. Cooperberg has expertise in various areas, including children and adolescents with AD/HD, autism spectrum disorders, and mood and behavioral disorders. He has conducted numerous evaluations and specializes in providing comprehensive psychoeducational and AD/HD evaluations. Dr. Cooperberg also provides individual and family therapy for people of all ages, as well as behavioral training for parents. He conducts weekly social skills training groups for children and adolescents. Dr. Cooperberg provides behavioral consultation to numerous school districts throughout the state of New Jersey, conducting functional behavioral assessments and providing assistance in writing behavior intervention plans.